ACADEMIC WORD POWER 1

ACADEMIC WORD POWER 1

Lisa Hollinger

Series editor: Donna Obenda
University of North Texas

Houghton Mifflin Company
Boston ▪ New York

Editor in Chief: *Patricia A. Coryell*
Director of ESL Publishing: *Susan Maguire*
Senior Development Editor: *Kathleen Sands-Boehmer*
Editorial Assistant: *Evangeline Bermas*
Cover Design Manager: *Diana Coe*
Marketing Manager: *Annamarie Rice*

Printed in the U.S.A.

Library of Congress Control Number: 2003103054

ISBN: 0-618-39768-X

1 2 3 4 5 6 7 8 9 - POO - 07 06 05 04 03

CONTENTS

UNIT 5

UNIT 6

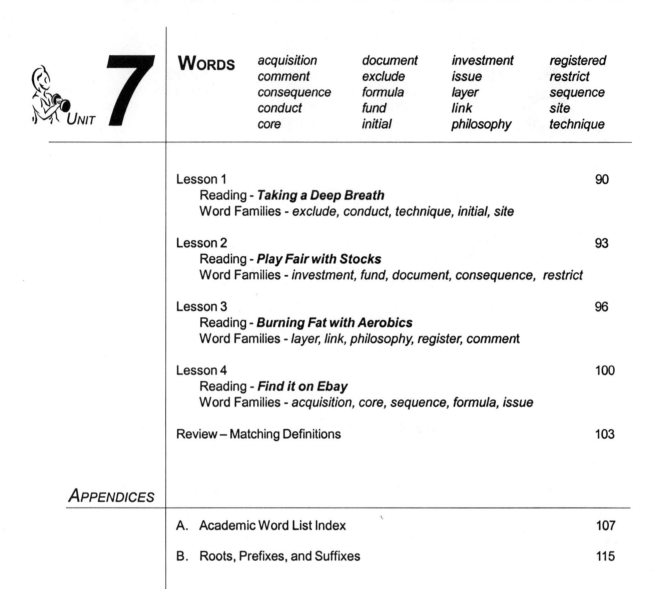

INTRODUCTION

WELCOME TO *ACADEMIC WORD POWER*!

ACADEMIC WORD POWER is a four-volume vocabulary series for students of English at the high school or college level who are planning to pursue further academic studies. The goal of the series is to help students learn the vocabulary they need for success in academic reading and writing.

ACADEMIC WORD POWER 1 is designed for intermediate students.

ACADEMIC WORD POWER 2, 3, and *4* are designed for high-intermediate, advanced, and high-advanced levels, respectively.

The target vocabulary in all four volumes was selected from the Academic Word List (AWL) developed by Averil Coxhead in 1998. The AWL, which contains 570 words, was compiled from a corpus of 3.5 million words found in academic texts. When students add the words from this list to a basic vocabulary of 2000 words, they will be able to comprehend approximately 90 percent of the vocabulary in academic texts. When proper nouns and technical vocabulary are added to this, students approach the 95 percent comprehension level that research has shown is needed for successful academic reading.

To the Teacher . . .

Series Approach

Reflecting the latest research in vocabulary acquisition and pedagogy, the exercises and activities in this text are based on an interactive approach to vocabulary instruction. Consequently, the reading, writing and speaking exercises give the student multiple exposures to the target words in meaningful contexts and provide rich information about each word. The exercises also establish ties between the target words and the student's prior knowledge and experience.

About the Books

Each volume has seven units that target 20 AWL words per unit. Thus, 140 AWL words are studied in each book, and 560 of the 570 words on the AWL are covered in the four volumes. The AWL words were sequenced and grouped into the four volumes by taking into consideration the frequency of the words, their level of difficulty and the thematic relationships between the words. A great variety of vocabulary development practice activities as well as strategies for learning and remembering academic vocabulary are incorporated in each book.

Text Organization

The seven units in each book are divided into four lessons that focus on five AWL words. Every lesson includes the following components:

- **Word Families**: This section introduces the five target words by providing a head word, which is the most frequently used in academic texts, as well as other word forms of the target word. A chart is provided for students to place the different word forms under the correct part of speech. This focus on word families helps students decipher new words and build spelling proficiency.

- **Reading**: A one-paragraph reading introduces students to the five target words in an academic context.

- **Comprehension Check:** Two exercises check students' superficial comprehension of the target words. For the first exercise, students match definitions by using the context provided in the reading in the previous section. The second exercise includes exercises such as true/false statements, yes/no questions, odd man out, fill in the blank, or matching sentence halves.

- **Word Study**: This section provides rich instruction through exercises that offer an expansion of the target words. This is accomplished through a wide variety of exercises, such as collocations, multiple meanings, grammar application, word form practice, analogies, pronunciation tips, and idiomatic usage. Both the written exercises in this section and the previous section are designed to be completed quickly by students and graded easily by teachers because research shows that the type of written exercise is not significant in terms of retention. Rather, it is the number of retrievals that is significant. Thus, it is better to have a larger quantity of exercises that can be done quickly as opposed to a smaller number of exercises that are time-consuming to complete (such as writing original sentences with the target words).

- **Using Words in Communication:** Communicative activities in this section give students practice in using the target words fluently. The students use the target words orally in different settings, such as sentence completion, discussion, role-play, interviewing, summariz ing, paraphrasing, storytelling, listing ideas related to the target word, or associating the target word with other words from the unit. These activities aid in retention of the target words as they develop a link between the target words and students' past experience and knowledge.

Other features of the series include:

- **Unit Reviews:** Each unit ends with an exercise that reviews all 20 words from the unit through an easy-to-do, fun activity, such as a crossword puzzle, find-a-word, word scramble, sentence scramble, associations, and definition match-up.

- **Website:** All four volumes have a companion website with an instructor and student site. This site can be accessed at www.college.hmco.com/esl. The instructor site includes unit assessments and the answer key for the book. The student site includes longer readings with the target AWL words, vocabulary flashcards, and review quizzes for each lesson.

- **Easy to supplement with writing activities**: If a teacher wants to do more extensive writing practice with the target words, the books can be easily supplemented with writing activities such as writing original sentences, paragraphs and essays with the AWL words.

TO THE STUDENT . . .

Did you know the following facts?

- The average native English-speaking university student has a vocabulary of around 21,000 words.

- The average adult ESL student learns about 2,500 English words per year.

Before you get depressed and discouraged, consider the following fact: English (like any other language) uses a relatively small number of words over and over again. Words that are used over and over again are called "high frequency" words. The words you will be studying in this book come from a high frequency list called the *Academic Word List* (AWL). The AWL contains 570 words that frequently occur in academic texts, such as university textbooks, course workbooks, and academic journal articles.

Why is it a good use of your time and energy to learn the words on the AWL?

If you add the 570 words on the AWL list to a basic vocabulary of 2000 English words (which most intermediate readers already have), you'll be able to understand 90% of the words in an average academic text. This book will help you learn many of the words on the AWL through numerous written exercises that introduce you to the meanings of the words and provide important information about the words, such as word forms, idiomatic uses, and pronunciation tips. This book also has many speaking activities that will give you practice using the new words fluently.

Besides completing all the exercises in the book, it is recommended that you use vocabulary cards to help you remember the new words. On the next page are some tips (advice) on how to make vocabulary cards.

HOW TO MAKE YOUR OWN VOCABULARY CARDS

1. Use small cards (no bigger than 3 by 5 inch) so that they can be easily carried.

2. Put the new word on one side and the definition (meaning) on the other side.

3. In addition to the definition, you can include the following information on the back side of the card:

    *   a translation of the new word in your language;
    *   pictures or diagrams related to the new word;
    *   phonetic pronunciation;
    *   a sample sentence using the new word.

4. Practice with the cards by looking at the new word and trying to recall the meaning first, and then (later) by looking at the meaning and trying to recall the new word.

5. Say the words aloud or to yourself when you are studying the cards.

6. Study the cards frequently. When you learn a new word, try to study it later that day, the next day, the next week, and then a few weeks later.

7. Study the words with a partner occasionally. When reviewing with a partner, try to use the word in a new sentence.

8. Change the order of the cards frequently. Don't order the cards alphabetically or put the cards in groups of similar words. Words which look the same or have similar meanings are easy to confuse.

GUIDE TO PRONUNCIATION

Vowels

Symbol	Key Word	Pronunciation
/ɑ/	hot	/hɑt/
/æ/	cat	/kæt/
/aɪ/	tie	/taɪ/
/aʊ/	cow	/kaʊ/
/ɛ/	bed	/bɛd/
/eɪ/	same	/seɪm/
/i/	he	/hɪ/
/ɪ/	it	/ɪt/
/oʊ/	go	/goʊ/
/ʊ/	book	/bʊk/
/ɔ/	dog	/dɔg/
/ɔɪ/	boy	/bɔɪ/
/ʌ/	cup	/kʌp/
/ɜr/	bird	/bɜrd/
/ə/	about	/əˈbaʊt/
	softer	/ˈsɔftər/

Consonants

Symbol	Key Word	Pronunciation
/b/	be	/bi/
/d/	did	/dɪd/
/dʒ/	jump	/dʒʌmp/
/f/	fat	/fæt/
/g/	go	/goʊ/
/h/	hit	/hɪt/
/k/	cat	/kæt/
/l/	life	/laɪf/
/m/	me	/mi/
/n/	no	/noʊ/
/ŋ/	sing	/sɪŋ/
/p/	pen	/pɛn/
/r/	red	/rɛd/
/s/	see	/si/
/t/	tea	/ti/
/tʃ/	cheap	/tʃip/
/v/	vote	/voʊt/
/w/	we	/wi/
/z/	zoo	/zʊ/
/ð/	they	/ðeɪ/
/θ/	thin	/θɪn/

GUIDE TO SYLLABLE STRESS

/ˈ/   open   /ˈoʊpən/
used before a syllable to show primary stress

/ˌ/   doorway   /ˈdɔrˌweɪ/
used before a syllable to show secondary stress

ACKNOWLEDGEMENTS

Many thanks to Averil Coxhead for giving us permission to use the *Academic Word List* (AWL) in the development of this series. It is hard to imagine the hours of planning and labor that went into compiling this list from such an extensive corpus (3.5 million running words from over 400 academic texts). For more information about the AWL see the article *A New Academic Word List* by Averil Coxhead in the Summer 2000 TESOL Quarterly.

Also, thanks to Barbara Hefka, an instructor at the University of North Texas Intensive English Language Institute (IELI) for sequencing and grouping the 570 words on the AWL for the four volumes in this series. When sequencing these words, Barbara had to take in consideration the frequency of the words, their level of difficulty, and thematic relationships between the words. It was a herculean task that only someone with Barbara's breadth of ESL experience and teaching intuition could have handled so well.

Huge thanks go to Judith Kulp, a publishing coordinator at UNT, for her invaluable, professional input on this project. Thanks also go to M. J. Weaver for her production skills, and to Yun Ju Kim, a communication design student at UNT, who created the graphics for the series.

Finally, thanks to Eva Bowman, Director of the IELI, and Dr. Rebecca Smith-Murdock, Director of International Programs, for their support in the development of the series. They had faith in my vision for the series and in the writing and creative abilities of the four authors: Lisa Hollinger, Celia Thompson, Pat Bull, and Barbara Jones.

- Donna Obenda

UNIT 1

WORDS

area	conclusion	final	occur
assist	cultural	identify	participation
available	define	method	physical
benefit	environment	minor	respond
community	factor	normally	similar

READINGS

Crime Fighters
Earthquake Insurance
The Smithsonian's New Kitchen
What's the Difference?

STRATEGIES AND SKILLS

Word Forms
- □ Word family chart
- □ Word form selection

Comprehension Check
- □ Matching definitions
- □ Identifying synonyms
- □ Understanding and using words in context

Word Expansion
- □ Collocations
- □ Grammar applications

Interactive Speaking Practice
- □ Sentence completion
- □ Listing
- □ Associations

ACADEMIC WORD POWER

LESSON 1

A. WORD FAMILIES

Study the five word families below. Then fill in the word form chart. The underlined word forms at the top of the list are the most commonly used forms in academic texts.

community	participation	factor (2X*)	cultural	response
/kəˈmyunəti/	/parˌtɪsəˈpeɪʃən/	/ˈfæktər/	/ˈkʌltʃərəl/	/rəˈspɑns/
	participate		culturally	respond
	participant		culture	respondent
	participatory		cultured	responsive
	participating			responsively

* used 2 times in the word form chart

Exercise - Word Form Chart

NOUN	VERB	ADJECTIVE	ADVERB
1. community			
1. participation 2.	1.	1. 2.	
1. factor	1.		
1.		1. cultural 2.	1.
1. response 2.	1.	1.	1.

B. READING

Crime Fighters

All across the United States, people of all social, <u>cultural</u>, and economic backgrounds are uniting to fight crime in their neighborhoods. That is why in many communities across the United States programs like Neighborhood Watch have been started. <u>Participation</u> in this program requires that a <u>community</u> of neighbors attend one meeting to get started. After that, all the neighbors put stickers in their front windows that alert possible criminals that this neighborhood is protected by a Neighborhood Watch program. That means that an individual member of the neighborhood agrees to call the police upon noticing any unusual activity. This can be a strong <u>factor</u> in reducing crime. Since this program was started, the <u>response</u> to it has been one of great interest. It's possible to see the stickers in homes all over the United States and even internationally. Grandmas and grandpas, moms and dads, aunts and uncles, and even kids get to feel like crime fighters!

C. COMPREHENSION CHECK

Exercise 1
Refer to the previous reading and use the context to guess the meanings of the words below. Then match the words to their definitions. Do NOT use a dictionary.

___ 1.	community	A.	taking part in an event or group
___ 2.	participation	B.	a social group sharing common interests
___ 3.	factor	C.	relating to the ideas, activities, and behavior of a specific group of people
___ 4.	cultural	D.	an answer
___ 5.	response	E.	element contributing to a particular result

Exercise 2
Which word does not belong?

1.	group	community	family	building
2.	factor	element	sister	part
3.	absence	sharing	involvement	participation
4.	reply	retort	respond	desist
5.	humanizing	cultural	civilizing	wild

D. WORD STUDY

Exercise 1
Many words in English are commonly used with certain prepositions. Find these words in the reading, and write the prepositions that go with them on the line provided. (Hint: One of the words has no preposition that goes with it.)

1. community _____
2. participation _____
3. factor _____
4. cultural _____
5. response _____

Exercise 2

"A factor in" versus **"To factor in."** Study the examples below.

Noun form	Class participation is an important **factor in** the learning process.
Verb form	When we analyze the state of the economy, we have to **factor in** the stock market as well as consumer spending.

Read the sentences below and decide whether **factor in** is used as a noun or a verb. Write N on the line if it's a noun and V if it's a verb.

___1. Losing his job is a major factor in Sam's current state of depression.

___2. Before we go on our vacation, we have to plan and factor in all the variables that could affect our trip, such as the weather and the amount of money we can spend.

___3. My math teacher told me that I failed the quiz because I forgot to factor in the right numbers.

___4. If you factor in the amount of money we spent on the treats, as well as the time spent creating the prizes, we put in a very big effort.

___5. One major factor in the war, which we have to consider, is geography.

E. USING WORDS IN COMMUNICATION

Exercise

Repeat and complete the following sentences.

1. An example of a <u>community</u> is...
2. <u>Participation</u> is required in ...
3. Some of the <u>factors</u> to consider when moving to a new country are...
4. <u>Cultural</u> activities in which I participate include...
5. If someone said hello to me, I might <u>respond</u> like this...

LESSON 2

A. WORD FAMILIES
Study the five word families below. Then fill in the word form chart. The underlined word forms at the top of the list are the most commonly used forms in academic texts.

environment	physical	normally	occur	minor (3X)
/ɛnˈvaɪrənmənt/	/ˈfɪzɪkəl/	/ˈnɔrməl/	/əˈkɜr/	/məˈnɔr/
environmental	physically	normal	occurrence	minority
environmentally		normalize		
environmentalist		abnormal		
		abnormality		

Exercise - Word Form Chart

NOUN	VERB	ADJECTIVE	ADVERB
1. environment 2.		1.	1.
		1. physical	1.
1.	1.	1. 2.	1. normally
1.	1. occur		
1. 2.	1.	1. minor	

B. READING

Earthquake Insurance

     Anyone who lives in California had better buy earthquake insurance. In most parts of California, <u>minor</u>, moderate, and major earthquakes <u>occur</u> frequently. <u>Normally</u>, a minor earthquake is nothing to worry about, but a moderate or major one can cause thousands of dollars worth of damage to your home. Because of this hazardous <u>environment</u>, homes in California are built with stronger <u>physical</u> structures than homes built elsewhere, but that doesn't protect a home completely. After the 1989 San Francisco earthquake that started during the third game of the World Series, the Association of California Insurance Companies said payment for damage reached two billion dollars.

C. COMPREHENSION CHECK
Exercise 1
Refer to the previous reading and use the context to guess the meanings of the words below. Then match the words to their definitions. Do NOT use a dictionary.

___1.	environment	A.	to happen
___2.	physical	B.	related to the body or material things
___3.	normally	C.	not important, small
___4.	occur	D.	external forces surrounding a creature
___5.	minor	E.	according to custom or habit

Exercise 2
True or False? Write T or F in the blanks provided.

___1.   A polluted city is an example of a healthy <u>environment</u> for humans.

___2.   A person's intelligence is an example of a <u>physical</u> trait.

___3.   A fire engine is <u>normally</u> red.

___4.   The Christmas holiday <u>occurs</u> only twice a year.

___5.   A <u>minor</u> earthquake often completely destroys a city.

D. WORD STUDY
Exercise
Choose the correct word form for each blank.

1. _____ are people who are concerned about the quality of the earth's air, land, and water.
   a. Environments   b. Environmentalists   c. Environmental

2. Doctors usually tell their patients that it is important to be _____ fit.
   a. physical   b. physically   c. physics

3. Peace agreements can help two warring countries _____ their relationship.
   a. normally   b. normal   c. normalize

4. On the night the accident _____ , Sam was at home asleep in bed.
   a. occurring   b. occurrence   c. occurred

5. Sara's college major was English, and her _____ was history.
   a. minority   b. minor   c. minors

E. USING WORDS IN COMMUNICATION
Exercise 1

1. List 3 <u>environments</u> in which humans might live.
2. List 3 <u>physical</u> characteristics that all humans possess.
3. List 3 foods you <u>normally</u> eat for breakfast.
4. List 3 events that <u>occur</u> in the Summer Olympics.
5. List 3 <u>minor</u> details of your partner's clothing.

Exercise 2
With a partner, discuss these questions.

1. Why do car accidents <u>occur</u>? Give some specific examples of how car accidents occur and how they could be avoided.
2. What do university students <u>normally</u> do when they graduate from university? Do you intend to do what's <u>normally</u> expected of a graduate?
3. Describe the <u>physical</u> characteristics of your mother or father. Do you share some of their <u>physical</u> characteristics? If so, which ones?
4. Many people today claim to be concerned about the <u>environment</u>; in other words, they care about the state of nature. They want clean air, unpolluted water, and pristine forests. Do you consider yourself to be an <u>environmentalist</u>? Why or why not?
5. People who are not old enough to drink alcohol legally are called <u>minors</u>. In your opinion, at what age is it reasonable to no longer be considered a <u>minor</u>?

LESSON 3

A. WORD FAMILIES

Study the five word families below. Then fill in the word form chart. The underlined word forms at the top of the list are the most commonly used forms in academic texts.

available	benefit (2X)	identify	method	assistance
/əˈveɪləbəl/	/ˈbɛnəˌfɪt/	/aɪˈdɛntəˌfaɪ/	/ˈmɛθəd/	/əˈsɪstəns/
availability	beneficial	identifiable	methodical	assist
unavailable	beneficiary	identifiably	methodology	assisted
unavailability		identification	methodically	assistant
		identity		

Exercise - Word Form Chart

NOUN	VERB	ADJECTIVE	ADVERB
1. 2.		1. available 2.	
1. 2.	1. benefit	1.	
1. 2.	1. identify	1.	1.
1. method 2.		1.	1.
1. assistance 2.	1.	1.	

B. READING

The Smithsonian's New Kitchen

There is a kitchen in one of the largest and most prestigious museums in the United States. Rather than being a place where food is cooked, this kitchen is on display. The Smithsonian's National Museum of American History has acquired the kitchen of famous chef Julia Child. Julia Child is one chef that most people, young or old, can <u>identify</u>. For 40 years, Julia Child gave <u>assistance</u> to the common person from that kitchen on her television show. She shared her <u>methods</u> for cooking with millions of people. Millions of families <u>benefited</u> from her techniques. What are her techniques? Rule number one: Use the freshest ingredients <u>available</u>. Unfortunately, just visiting this exhibit in Washington, D.C., won't make a person into a great chef.

C. COMPREHENSION CHECK
Exercise 1
Refer to the previous reading and use the context to guess the meanings of the words below. Then match the words to their definitions. Do NOT use a dictionary.

____1. available   A. to clearly state what something is
____2. benefit   B. aid; help in doing something
____3. identify   C. a way of doing something
____4. method   D. able to be used or seen
____5. assistance   E. to gain from something

Exercise 2
Yes or No? Answer the questions with YES or NO.

____1. Is cycling a <u>method</u> of transportation?
____2. Is assistance <u>available</u> to students with disabilities at public schools?
____3. Can you <u>identify</u> a criminal by his fingerprints?
____4. Do teacher's office hours usually <u>benefit</u> students?
____5. Does a bad son <u>assist</u> his father?

D. WORD STUDY
Exercise
In the English language, certain words are used together regularly and sound correct together. These are called collocations. For example, a common collocation with <u>method</u>, one of the words from Unit 1, is <u>scientific method</u>. Look at the other collocations for the words from this unit. Try to guess the correct answers focusing on the meanings you've learned for the vocabulary words in this unit.

scientific method	positively identify	available for hire
social benefit	assisted living	

Circle the letter of the correct answers for these collocations.

1. If a scientist uses the <u>scientific method</u> to prove her hypothesis, what steps must she follow?
    a. do experiments, accept or reject the hypothesis, publish the results
    b. find an animal, cut it up, photograph its organs
    c. build a spaceship, fill it with jet fuel, launch it into space

2. Which of the following is a <u>social benefit</u> of living in a dormitory?
    a. eating cafeteria food
    b. making new friends
    c. studying in your room

3. What characteristics can be used to <u>positively identify</u> a suspect in a crime?
   a. fingerprints and DNA
   b. size and color of clothing
   c. membership in a particular club

4. Which segment of the population might require <u>assisted living</u>?
   a. young married couples
   b. professional athletes
   c. the elderly (i.e., people over the age of 65)

5. Which of the following might be <u>available for hire</u>?
   a. a hospital
   b. a private detective
   c. an insect

E. USING WORDS IN COMMUNICATION
Exercise 1
Role Play - You and your partner must give some advice to a new English teacher using these words: **available, benefit, identify, method,** and **assist.** You may wish to write your role play as a dialog and then perform it aloud.

Exercise 2
Read and complete the following.

1. If I got a part-time job, I would be <u>available</u> to work...
2. The greatest <u>benefit</u> of studying abroad is...
3. Everyone should be able to <u>identify</u>...
4. A <u>method</u> should be developed for...
5. The last time I offered <u>assistance</u> to someone was...

LESSON 4

A. WORD FAMILIES
Study the five word families below. Then fill in the word form chart. The underlined word forms at the top of the list are the most commonly used forms in academic texts.

final	conclusion	similar	definition	area
/ˈfaɪnl/	/kənˈkluːʒən/	/ˈsɪmələr/	/ˌdɛfəˈnɪʃən/	/ˈɛriə/
finalize	conclude	dissimilar	definable	
finalized	conclusive	similarity	define	
finally	inconclusive	similarly	undefined	
finality	conclusively		definably	

Exercise - Word Form Chart

NOUN	VERB	ADJECTIVE	ADVERB
1.	1.	1. final 2.	1.
1. conclusion	1.	1. 2.	1.
1.		1. similar 2.	1.
1. definition	1.	1. 2.	1.
1. area			

B. READING

What's the Difference?

Vocabulary building is an <u>area</u> of study that can be difficult for students due to the thousands of synonyms in the English language. It can be confusing, especially when trying to understand small differences between words that have <u>similar</u> meanings. Understanding word forms can assist students in this task. For example, the words *final* and *conclusion* have similar <u>definitions</u>. *Final* means last and is an adjective that is sometimes used like a noun. For example, instead of saying *final exams*, it has become commonplace to say *finals*. *Conclusion*, on the other hand, is a noun, which means the end of something. It can never be used as an adjective. Therefore, one must focus on word form when making a distinction between these two words.

C. COMPREHENSION CHECK
Exercise 1
Refer to the previous reading and use the context to guess the meanings of the words below. Then match the words to their definitions. Do NOT use a dictionary.

___1.	final	A.	the meaning
___2.	conclusion	B.	ending
___3.	similar	C.	a place or part of the world
___4.	definition	D.	last
___5.	area	E.	having a likeness

Exercise 2
Choose the word that is different in meaning.

1.	final	conclusion	area	end
2.	similar	like	weak	resembling
3.	conclude	define	identify	point out

D. WORD STUDY
Exercise
Choose the correct word form for each blank.

1. We have _____ exams at the end of each term.
   a. finally   b. final   c. finalize

2. The police had to let the suspect go free because they did not have evidence which could be considered _____.
   a. conclusion   b. conclude   c. conclusive

3. Crocodiles and alligators have many_____ characteristics.
   a. similar   b. similarly   c. similarity

4. Webster decided to attempt to _____ every word in the English language.
   a. define   b. definition   c. defining

5. There are many _____ of concentration within the discipline of education.
   a. area   b. areas   c. aerial

E. USING WORDS IN COMMUNICATION

Exercise 1

Word Associations - On a sheet of paper, write down several words that you associate with each of these five keywords. When you finish, cut up the lists and give them to your partner. She/He will give you hers/his. Try to place the associated words under the correct keywords. Compare and discuss.

For example, you might associate **similar** with **different.**

Exercise 2

With a partner, discuss the following:

1. The <u>final</u> days of preparation before leaving home can be very difficult. What were some of the <u>final</u> details you attended to before you took your last trip?

2. Why do you think it is important for a story to have a <u>conclusion</u>? What kinds of <u>conclusions</u> do you like to read (i.e., happy endings, unresolved mysteries, etc.)? Why?

3. In what ways are you <u>similar</u> to your parents? To your brothers and sisters?

4. How do you <u>define</u> success? Why are <u>definitions</u> important?

5. If you could travel to any <u>area</u> of the world, where would you like to go? Why would you choose that <u>area</u>?

REVIEW

The crossword puzzle below contains all 20 words from Unit 1. Solve the puzzle by filling in the blanks to complete the sentences on the next page.

ACROSS

2. The _____ exam is given in the last week of the term.

5. I can't do this all alone. You must _____ me so that I can do it correctly.

8. Trust is an important _____ in a successful relationship.

9. Art and literature are two examples of _____ works.

11. I left out the _____ details because I didn't think they were important enough to mention.

13. I tried to book a flight on a plane to Timbuktu, but there weren't any seats _____ .

14. When did the accident _____ ? Was it on Tuesday or Wednesday?

15. How do you _____ "war"? What is it exactly?

18. We don't _____ stay our late on weekdays because we have to wake up early in the morning.

DOWN

1. The money that you give to the Red Cross will _____ the victims of the tragedy.

3. In order to build an airport, a city needs a large _____ of land.

4. Doctors take care of our _____ needs, and holy men take care of our spiritual concerns.

6. They are fraternal twins, so they don't look exactly alike, but they do look _____ to each other.

7. African villages are famous for their wonderful sense of _____ ; everybody looks out for each other.

9. At the _____ of the book, the hero kills the monster and marries the beautiful maiden.

10. I asked him a question, but he didn't _____ . I wonder if he heard me.

12. Your _____ in class is key to a good grade.

16. The mortuary asked the parents to _____ the body of their dead son.

17. The World Wildlife Fund champions the natural _____ so that wild animals can have a place to live on this planet.

19. In order to be efficient about this, we're going to have to develop a _____ .

UNIT 2

WORDS

achieve	create	involved	required
affect	emphasis	major	section
approach	evaluation	partnership	task
chapter	individual	percent	traditional
context	injury	process	variable

READINGS

Save Your Dictionary
Denmark's Elves
A Realistic Look at Marriage
Will She Wear White?

STRATEGIES AND SKILLS

Word Forms
- □ Word family chart
- □ Word form selection

Comprehension Check
- □ Matching definitions
- □ Identifying synonyms
- □ Understanding and Using words in context

Word Expansion
- □ Collocations
- □ Listing

Interactive Speaking Practice
- □ Sentence completion
- □ Listing
- □ Interviewing
- □ Summarizing
- □ Role play

ACADEMIC WORD POWER

LESSON 1

A. WORD FAMILIES

Study the five word families below. Then fill in the word form chart. The underlined word forms at the top of the list are the most commonly used forms in academic texts.

achieve	affect	approach (2X)	chapter	context
/əˈtʃiv/	/əˈfɛkt/	/əˈproutʃ/	/ˈtʃæptər/	/ˈkɑnˌtɛkst/
achievement	affected	approaching		contextual
achievable	affective	approachable		contextualize
	affectively	unapproachable		contextualized
	unaffected			uncontextualized

Exercise - Word Form Chart

NOUN	VERB	ADJECTIVE	ADVERB
1.	1. achieve	1.	
	1. affect	1. 2. 3.	1.
1. approach	1.	1. 2. 3.	
1. chapter			
1. context	1.	1. 2. 3.	

B. READING

Save your Dictionary!

College textbooks can be overwhelming to students coming out of high school. The ability to use certain reading skills, such as guessing vocabulary from <u>context</u>, can be a real asset. Without skills such as those, some students will find it difficult to <u>achieve</u> their goal of graduating from college. The quality of a high school education directly <u>affects</u> a person's ability to read and comprehend a book that has numerous <u>chapters</u> and uses high-level vocabulary. Some students get stuck looking up every word they don't know. This can take hours. One of the best <u>approaches</u> for reading college texts is to guess the new words from <u>context</u>. Using the surrounding words to get a general idea of the word is far superior to wearing out the dictionary.

C. COMPREHENSION CHECK

Exercise 1

Refer to the reading above and use the context to guess the meanings of the words below. Then match the words to their definitions. Do not use a dictionary.

____1. achieve
____2. affect

____3. approaches
____4. chapter
____5. context

A. one of the main divisions of a book
B. the information around a word that helps determine the meaning
C. to influence
D. courses of action, methods
E. to reach, gain, acquire

Exercise 2

If the underlined word is used correctly in the sentence write YES in the blank. If it is not used correctly write NO.

____1. Students who never study can <u>achieve</u> a lot of academic success.
____2. The President gave a moving speech that <u>affected</u> all the citizens.
____3. One <u>approach</u> to making a difficult decision is to list the pros and cons.
____4. It takes many books to comprise one <u>chapter</u>.
____5. Using <u>context</u> to guess unknown words while reading can facilitate comprehension.

D. WORD STUDY

Exercise 1

Many words have more than one meaning.
Consider these four meanings of the word **approach.**

1. approach(v) – to begin to handle a situation.

2. approach (v) – to come near or nearer (to).

3. approach(v) – to speak to, esp. about something for the first time.

4. approach(n) – a course of action.

Read the sentences below and decide if the meaning is 1, 2, 3, or 4.

____ 1. He becomes nervous when <u>approaching</u> women.
____ 2. We must take shelter since the storm is <u>approaching</u>.
____ 3. What is the best way to <u>approach</u> the problem?
____ 4. The scientist was uncertain about what <u>approach</u> to use in proving her hypothesis.
____ 5. When one is <u>approaching</u> an unknown animal, it's best to use caution.

Exercise 2
Consider these three meanings of the verb **affect**.

---

1. affect – to have an influence on

   example: The amount of effort put into any task usually <u>affects</u> the outcome.

2. affect – to pretend or simulate

   example: The American <u>affected</u> a Russian accent in order to appear to be Russian.

3. affect – to touch one's emotions

   example: The father was greatly <u>affected</u> by the birth of his first daughter.

Read the sentences below and decide if the meaning of the verb is 1, 2, or 3.

___ 1.   Drinking alcohol can <u>affect</u> your ability to drive.

___ 2.   Don't <u>affect</u> a sweet and innocent face when I'm punishing you.

___ 3.   Everyone was surprised at the tricky salesman's ability to <u>affect</u> an honest character.

___ 4.   Culture shock often <u>affects</u> a student's ability to perform well in class.

___ 5.   The professor was deeply <u>affected</u> by the news of the accident.

E. USING WORDS IN COMMUNICATION
Exercise
Repeat and complete the following sentences.

1.   In my life I want to <u>achieve</u>....

2.   The weather <u>affects</u> me in these ways...

3.   The best way to <u>approach</u> a serious problem is...

4.   For me, using <u>context</u> to guess the meaning of new words is...

LESSON 2

A. WORD FAMILIES

Study the five word families below. Then fill in the word form chart. The underlined word forms at the top of the list are the most commonly used forms in academic texts.

create	emphasis	evaluation	individual	injury
<u>create</u>	<u>emphasis</u>	<u>evaluation</u>	<u>individual</u>	<u>injury</u>
/kri'eɪt/	/'ɛmfəsɪs/	/ɪˌvælyu'eɪʃən/	/ˌndə'vɪdʒuəl/	/'ndʒəri/
creation	emphasize	evaluate	individualize	injure
creative	emphatic	evaluative	individually	injured
creatively	emphatically	re-evaluate	individualist	injurious
creativity		re-evaluation	individualism	uninjured
creator			individuality	
recreate			individualistic	

Exercise - Word Form Chart

NOUN	VERB	ADJECTIVE	ADVERB
1. 2. 3.	1. create 2.	1.	1.
1. emphasis	1.	1.	1.
1. evaluation 2.	1. 2.	1.	
1. individual 2. 3. 4.	1.	1.	1.
1. injury	1.	1. 2. 3.	

B. READING

Denmark's Elves

Children in the U.S. learn about Santa, the North Pole, and the elves who work there. At a very young age, their parents help <u>create</u> the belief that on Christmas Eve Santa comes down the chimney bringing gifts. In contrast, in Denmark, children don't wait for Santa, but for elves (little, old men). There, the <u>emphasis</u> is placed on these elves, called *nissen*. Perhaps an evaluation of the two folklores is necessary. It seems more likely that many elves could deliver presents to the world more effectively than one <u>individual</u>, especially when that individual happens to be overweight. Santa might be too big to get down the chimney without causing <u>injury</u> to himself, while the little elves of Denmark could manage it nicely.

C. COMPREHENSION CHECK
Exercise 1
Refer to the previous reading and use the context to guess the meanings of the words below. Then match the words to their definitions. Do NOT use a dictionary.

____ 1. create		A.	special importance placed on something
____ 2. emphasis		B.	a wound or damage
____ 3. evaluation		C.	a calculation of value or worth
____ 4. individual		D.	a single person; considered separately
____ 5. injury		E.	to cause to exist; originate

Exercise 2
Which word does not belong?

1.	originate	make	supply	create
2.	importance	minor	emphasis	focus
3.	evaluation	composition test	quiz	listening practice
4.	single	individual	people	one
5.	harm	hurt	injury	improve

D. WORD STUDY
Exercise
Choose the correct word form for each blank.

1. Students who have a lot of _____ usually write the most interesting compositions.
   a. creative   b. creatively   c. creativity

2. She was extremely _____ about her choice for the prize.
   a. emphasize   b. emphatic   c. emphatically

3. Teachers use many tools to _____ their students' progress.
   a. evaluate   b. evaluation   c. evaluative

4. _____ is an ideal that most Americans believe in.
   a. individualize   b. individual   c. individualism

5. In a lawsuit, the _____ party must provide evidence that the defendant is guilty.
   a. injuring   b. injured   c. injuries

E. USING WORDS IN COMMUNICATION
Exercise 1

1. List 3 ways to <u>create</u> a cleaner world.
2. List 3 areas on which teachers should place <u>emphasis</u>.
3. List 3 of the best methods to <u>evaluate</u> students' skills.
4. List 3 <u>individuals</u> who achieved great success in life.
5. List 3 <u>injuries</u> that you have had in your life.

Exercise 2

With a partner, discuss these questions.

1. Discuss the most serious <u>injury</u> in your life. How were you <u>injured</u>? Research shows that smoking is <u>injurious</u> to your health. Why do you think so many people choose to smoke despite the health risks?

2. Are you an <u>individualist</u>? Are people in your family <u>individualistic</u>? Do you think <u>individualism</u> is important, or is it more important to conform?

3. Discuss the three methods of <u>evaluating</u> students. How do you prefer to have your skills <u>evaluated</u>? In what cases is it fair to request a <u>reevaluation</u> of your skills?

4. When you were growing up, what ideals did your parents <u>emphasize</u>? Which rules were they very <u>emphatic</u> about? Did you agree? Why or why not?

5. Do you like to <u>create</u> things? Do you consider yourself a <u>creative</u> person? In what ways? How can you improve your <u>creativity</u>?

LESSON 3

A. WORD FAMILIES
Study the five word families below. Then fill in the word form chart. The underlined word forms at the top of the list are the most commonly used forms in academic texts.

involve	major (3X)	partnership	percent	process (2X)
/ɪnˈvɑlv/	/ˈmeɪdʒər/	/ˈpɑrtnərˌʃɪp/	/pərˈsɛnt/	/ˈprɑˌsɛs/
involved	majority	partner	percentage	processed
uninvolved				
involvement				

Exercise - Word Form Chart

NOUN	VERB	ADJECTIVE	ADVERB
1.	1. involve	1. 2.	
1. 2.	1.	1. major	
1. partnership 2.			
1.			1. percent
1. process	1.	1.	

B. READING

A Realistic Look at Marriage

Young couples getting married think they will be sitting side by side in rocking chairs in 60 years. However, statistics about divorce show a startling fact: Fifty <u>percent</u> of all marriages in the U.S. end in divorce. Unfortunately, that statistic seems to be on the rise. Why do so many marriages fail? One <u>major</u> reason is that even though they are married, they feel a lack of <u>partnership</u> in the marriage. That is to say that one or both members are not <u>involved</u> in the marriage equally. Another reason might be that the <u>process</u> of divorce has become simpler. The steps involved are much easier and less time consuming than in the past, so one might think it's easier just to get divorced than to work on the marriage.

C. COMPREHENSION CHECK
Exercise 1
Refer to the previous reading and use the context to guess the meanings of the words below. Then match the words to their definitions. Do NOT use a dictionary.

___1. involved

A. a series of steps used to get some result, a specific method

___2. major

B. for or out of each hundred

___3. partnership

C. to be a part of

___4. percent

D. greater in importance

___5. process

E. two or more people associated in a common activity

Exercise 2
Choose from the words above to fill in the blanks.

1. Some loans charge up to 8 _____ interest per year.
2. If a person wants to affect the political situation in his or her country, it's necessary to become _____ in politics in some way.
3. Having the motor replaced in your car is a _____ car repair.
4. The NATO Alliance is a _____ designed to protect the participating nations.
5. Applying and being accepted to graduate school is a long and difficult _____.

D. WORD STUDY
Exercise
Select the pair of words having a similar relationship as the **boldfaced** pair.

____1. **involved : included** : :

a. desired : hated
b. creative : emphatic
c. evaluation : test

____2. **major : minor** : :

a. individualist : conformist
b. chapter : section
c. achieve : accomplish

____3. **partner : partnership** : :

a. affect : approach
b. individual : society
c. context : creative

____4. **percent : part of 100** : :

a. succeed : fail
b. emphasize : emphatic
c. chapter : main division of a book

____5. **process : processed** : :

a. evaluate : create
b. injury : injured
c. affected : unaffected

E. USING WORDS IN COMMUNICATION
Exercise 1
Repeat and complete the following sentences.

1. In high school, I was <u>involved</u> in...
   Now I am <u>involved</u> in...
2. In the future, my college <u>major</u> will be...
   A popular <u>major</u> around the world is...
3. Two countries that have a <u>partnership</u> are...
   Two countries that could benefit from a <u>partnership</u> are...
4. I am 100 <u>percent</u> satisfied with...
   I am not 100 <u>percent</u> satisfied with...
5. A difficult <u>process</u> is...
   An easy <u>process</u> is...

Exercise 2
Using these vocabulary words from this lesson, write questions to interview a classmate about his/her academic plans.

1. **involved**
2. **major**
3. **partnership**
4. **percent**
5. **process**

LESSON 4

A. WORD FAMILIES
Study the five word families below. Then fill in the word form chart. The underlined word
forms at the top of the list are the most commonly used forms in academic texts.

require	section	task	traditional	variable
/rəˈkwaɪrd/	/ˈsɛkʃən/	/tæsk/	/trəˈdɪʃənəl/	/ˈvɛriəbəl/
required	sectioned		tradition	vary
requirement			traditionalist	varied
			traditionally	varying
			non-traditional	variation
				variably
				invariably

Exercise - Word Form Chart

NOUN	VERB	ADJECTIVE	ADVERB
1.	1. require	1.	
1. section		1.	
1. task			
1. 2.		1. traditional 2.	1.
1. variable 2.	1.	1. 2.	1. 2.

B. READING

Will She Wear White?

We can all envision the <u>traditional</u> wedding gown. It's long, silk, and decorated with
lace or pearls. The dress has a veil to go with it and a train to drag behind it. Most impor-
tantly, it's white. Currently, however, there are more and more <u>variables</u> in people's lives and
their weddings. This might not be the first wedding, it might be a casual wedding, or it might
be a wedding of people who have lived together for years. However, there is still a certain
<u>section</u> of the population that believes white is <u>required</u> for a first wedding and that a bride
should wear a different color for the second or third wedding. Nevertheless, this traditional
belief is fading, leaving the wedding dress choice and the <u>task</u> of finding the perfect dress up
to the bride.

C. COMPREHENSION CHECK
Exercise 1
Refer to the previous reading and use the context to guess the meanings of the words below. Then match the words to their definitions. Do NOT use a dictionary.

____ 1. required   A. a part or subdivision
____ 2. section   B. needed; demanded
____ 3. task   C. things that can change
____ 4. traditional   D. time-honored; passed down
____ 5. variables   E. work; job

Exercise 2
Is the underlined word used correctly in the situation? Write YES or NO.

____ 1. When making an important decision, it's best to consider all the variables.
____ 2. Beer is a required part of any diet.
____ 3. Young people in the U.S.A. are becoming less and less traditional.
____ 4. I received a task for my birthday.
____ 5. Each section of an orange could contain seeds.

D. WORD STUDY
Exercise
These are some common collocations for the words in this lesson.

task force	traditional social values
required courses	patient variables

Answer the following questions based on these collocations by circling the letter of the correct answer.

1. When a task force is formed, what can we expect this group to do?
   a. attend social events together
   b. work together to accomplish some goal
   c. take classes about the forces of nature together

2. What can we expect of an American with traditional social values?
   a. The person will agree with polygamy (having more than one wife).
   b. The person will have had children but never have gotten married.
   c. The person believes in marriage between one man and one woman.

3. If doctors are discussing the difficulty of patient variables in planning a treatment program, what might they be worried about?
   a. the different lifestyles of patients
   b. transportation of the patients to the hospital
   c. the different medications available for a certain disease

4. What does it mean if an undergraduate student must complete his or her required courses by junior year?
   a. The student must finish certain classes before starting the third year of college.
   b. The student must declare a major before completing elective classes.
   c. The student can wait to take the basic requirements until he or she is a senior.

E. USING WORDS IN COMMUNICATION

Exercise 1

Reread the paragraph from this lesson. After two minutes, close your book and summarize the paragraph to your partner. Try to use as many vocabulary words as possible.

Exercise 2

Role Play - You and a partner will create and perform a role play in front of the class. You should make a script and practice before presenting. Use as many words from the unit as possible.

Student A: You are a student getting ready to enter the university. You have a meeting with an advisor to discuss your deficiencies, plan for study, paperwork you must complete, and different paths you can take. Use as many of the vocabulary words from the unit as you can.

Student B: You are an advisor at the university meeting with a student to discuss his/her future enrollment. Use as many words from the unit as possible in your conversation with the student. Make a plan with suggestions about how to complete the necessary steps in the process of enrollment.

REVIEW

Choose any five words from this unit and write one in each oval. Then write any four words that you associate with those words on the extending lines. Be able to explain your associations to a partner. (See the example at right.)

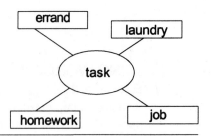

1.

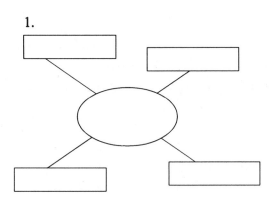

2.

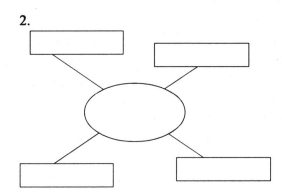

3.

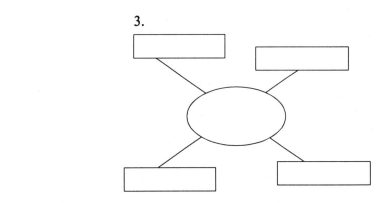

4.

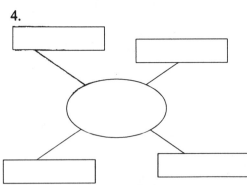

5.

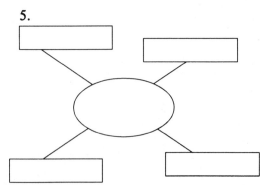

UNIT 3

WORDS

appropriate	design	maintenance	select
concept	element	policy	significant
consumer	evidence	positive	survey
credit	focus	region	technology
data	interaction	security	text

READINGS
Credit Card Danger
Tattoo Trouble
Secure Your Computer
Shop 'Til You Drop

STRATEGIES AND SKILLS
Word Forms
- Word family chart
- Word form selection

Comprehension Check
- Matching definitions
- Identifying synonyms
- Understanding words in context

Word Expansion
- Multiple meanings
- Collocations
- Idiomatic usage

Interactive Speaking Practice
- Sentence completion
- Designing a survey
- Paraphrasing

ACADEMIC WORD POWER

LESSON 1

A. WORD FAMILIES

Study the five word families below. Then fill in the word form chart. The underlined word forms at the top of the list are the most commonly used forms in academic texts.

consumer	positive	appropriate	credit (2X)	focus (2X)
/kəˈsumər/	/ˈpɑzətɪv/	/əˈpoʊpriɪt/	/ˈkrɛdɪt/	/ˈfoʊkəs/
consume	positively	appropriately	creditor	focused
consumption		appropriateness		refocus
		inappropriate		
		inappropriately		

Exercise - Word Form Chart

NOUN	VERB	ADJECTIVE	ADVERB
1. consumer 2.	1.		
		1. positive	1.
1.		1. appropriate 2.	1. 2.
1. credit 2.	1.		
1.	1. focus 2.	1.	

B. READING

Credit Card Danger

Credit cards are easily accessible in the United States. Credit card companies are constantly sending attractive offers to students in college. They encourage students to sign up now and pay no interest for a year! What they hope is that students will build a large debt on their cards and still be paying for it in a year, this time WITH interest. As a matter of fact, credit card companies focus much of their advertising on students for that very reason. Many economists question whether or not it is appropriate to offer this huge responsibility to young consumers who have little or no income. By the time many students graduate, they must get a job immediately to pay their credit card bills. If they can't pay them, they start off life with a negative credit history instead of a positive one. This can affect the ability to get loans for homes or cars later in life. Students would be wise to throw away those flashy offers for credit cards.

C. COMPREHENSION CHECK
Exercise 1
Refer to the previous reading and use the context to guess the meanings of the words below. Then match the words to their definitions. Do NOT use a dictionary.

___ 1. consumer   A. correct, suitable
___ 2. positive   B. the person who buys and uses goods and services
___ 3. appropriate   C. optimistic, hopeful
___ 4. credit   D. the ability to buy now and pay later
___ 5. focus   E. to center one's attention on

Exercise 2
Which word does not belong?

1. consumer	buyer	seller	user
2. pessimistic	positive	good	optimistic
3. right	correct	unsuitable	appropriate
4. credit	loan	cash	borrowed money
5. daydream	concentrate	focus	pay attention

D. WORD STUDY
Exercise 1
Many words in English have more than one meaning.
Consider these different meanings of the word **credit**.

1. credit (n) – the ability to buy now and pay later
2. credit (n) - a cause for admiration, honor or praise
3. credit (n) – a unit of a course at school
4. credit (v) – to express admiration for someone
5. credit (v) – to add a sum to someone's account

Read the sentences below and decide which meaning is expressed. Write 1, 2, 3, 4, or 5 on the line provided.

___ 1. When I sent a $300 dollar check, Visa credited my account.
___ 2. Give the teacher credit for explaining the concept so clearly.
___ 3. It's common for an undergraduate student to take 12 credit hours, but a graduate student usually takes 9.
___ 4. We credit the fire fighters and other emergency personnel for saving many lives during the attack.
___ 5. He was able to get the loan easily because he has good credit.

Exercise 2

These are some common collocations for the words in this unit.

consumer confidence	positive outlook	appropriate behavior
currently focusing	credit limit	

Circle the letter of the correct answer for these collocations.

1. If <u>consumer confidence</u> is low, that means…
   a. people are willing to spend money and go into debt
   b. people want to sell all their belongings
   c. people are conservative about spending and try to save money instead

2. People with <u>positive outlooks</u> think…
   a. it's better to be safe than sorry
   b. the best is bound to happen
   c. bad luck will follow them

3. If you want to exhibit <u>appropriate behavior</u> in class, you should…
   a. stand up and shout
   b. speak to others while the teacher is speaking
   c. raise your hand to ask or answer a question

4. If the U.S. government is <u>currently focusing</u> on domestic problems, they are…
   a. passing legislation dealing with situations in the U.S.A.
   b. passing legislation dealing with foreign trade
   c. not passing any legislation

5. When you meet your <u>credit limit</u> on your credit card,…
   a. you must throw it away
   b. you can't use it until you pay some of the balance
   c. you can stop making payments and cancel the card

E. USING WORDS IN COMMUNICATION
Exercise
Repeat and complete the following sentences.

1. Advertising affects <u>consumers</u> by…
2. <u>Appropriate</u> clothing for a wedding is…
3. Something I feel very <u>positive</u> about is…
4. In order to <u>focus</u> on my homework, I…
5. If I could get a million dollar <u>credit</u> line, I would…

LESSON 2

A. WORD FAMILIES

Study the five word families below. Then fill in the word form chart. The underlined word forms at the top of the list are the most commonly used forms in academic texts.

survey (2X)	design (2X)	select (2x)	data	text
/'sərveɪ/	/dɪzaɪn/	/sə'lɛkt/	/deɪtə/	/tɛkst/
surveyed	designer	selection	/dætə/	textual
		selective		
		selectively		

Exercise - Word Form Chart

NOUN	VERB	ADJECTIVE	ADVERB
1. survey	1.	1.	
1. 2.	1. design		
1.	1. select	1. 2.	1.
1. data			
1. text		1.	

B. READING

Tattoo Trouble

Years ago, it was rare to find someone with a tattoo. Nowadays, if you did a <u>survey</u>, you might find that large numbers of students, young adults, and even older adults <u>select</u> to have their bodies marked with tattoos. It is possible to <u>design</u> your own picture or choose a design that the tattoo artist has on file in the studio. You might even want to have some <u>text</u> tattooed on you, like your girlfriend's name or a word that has meaning to you. The problem comes when you and your girlfriend break up. Now you have to get that tattoo removed. This is where the Food and Drug Administration (FDA) has stepped in. The FDA is currently collecting <u>data</u> on problems with tattoos. The main areas of concern are infection, removal problems, and allergic reactions. Over 50 different dyes are used in tattooing, and none of them has been approved for injection into the skin of humans by the FDA. In the future, it may become more difficult to get the tattoo of your choice.

C. COMPREHENSION CHECK
Exercise 1
Refer to the previous reading at the beginning of the unit and use the context to guess the meanings of the words below. Then match the words to their definitions. Do NOT use a dictionary.

_____ 1. survey   A. to choose

_____ 2. design   B. information

_____ 3. select   C. a set of questions about opinions

_____ 4. data   D. written material

_____ 5. text   E. to draw sketches or make plans for

Exercise 2
True or False? Write T or F in the blanks provided.

_____ 1. A <u>survey</u> is non-informative.

_____ 2. You should look at many possible houses before you <u>select</u> a home.

_____ 3. Most <u>data</u> tells us nothing.

_____ 4. Graduate school books often contain complex <u>text</u>.

_____ 5. It takes a lot of work to <u>design</u> an advertising campaign.

D. WORD STUDY
Exercise
Some words have the same form in noun or verb form. The spelling is the same, but the meaning and pronunciation can be different. Study the meanings of the noun and verb forms of **survey** below.

---

survey (n)   /ˈsɜrˌveɪ/

1. survey (n) – a set of questions designed to measure the opinions of people

2. survey (n) – a general view or examination of a place

survey (v)   /sərˈveɪ/

3. survey (v) – to examine the opinions of a group of people

4. survey (v) – to examine the condition of something

Use the definitions of **survey** on the previous page to choose the appropriate meaning and form of the word. Put the number of the definition in the first blank provided and write the word in the next blank. Be sure to change verb forms if necessary.

___ 1. He _____ his finances before buying a new car.

___ 2. Before and after each election, the polling company _____ the public.

___ 3. When designing a _____, it's important to consider the reading abilities of your respondents.

___ 4. Our _____ of the company revealed that it was in trouble.

E. USING WORDS IN COMMUNICATION
Exercise 1
With a partner, discuss these questions.

1. Have you ever participated in a survey? Have you ever conducted a survey? Describe it and explain the opinions you gave or were given.

2. Do you like to design things? What kind of things do you design? Who is your favorite clothing designer? Why?

3. How did you select this school? What factors affected your selection? Were you very selective, or did you just choose quickly?

4. What is the best way to collect data? (by telephone, mail, e-mail, surveyors in malls, (etc.) How do you feel when someone tries to collect data from you? Is there any data that you would refuse to provide?

5. What kind of text do you prefer to read? Describe text that is the most enjoyable, easiest to read, clearest to see, etc. Do you like to read text on-line? Why or why not?

Exercise 2
You and a partner will design a survey to collect data to help in the selection of new school rules regarding absences. You will make decisions about the design of the survey, what kind of text will be included, whom you will survey (i.e. students, teachers, administrators), and how you will select the new policy based on the data. Discuss how you will go about this process.

Things to consider:

How long will the survey be? What kind of questions will you ask? Who will you talk to? How can you be sure it is a fair evaluation of the major opinions on campus? How can you analyze the data after you collect it? Whose opinion has more weight in the selection process?

LESSON 3

A. WORD FAMILIES

Study the five word families below. Then fill in the word form chart. The underlined word forms at the top of the list are the most commonly used forms in academic texts.

security	technology	interaction	maintenance	evidence
/sə'kyʊrəti/	/tɛk'nɑlədʒi/	/ˌɪntər'ækʃən/	/'meɪntənəns/	/'ɛvədəns/
secure (2X)	technological	interact	maintain	evident
securely	technologically	interactive	maintained	evidential
insecure		interactively		evidently
insecurity				

Exercise - Word Form Chart

NOUN	VERB	ADJECTIVE	ADVERB
1. security 2.	1.	1. 2.	1.
1. technology		1.	1.
1. interaction	1.	1.	1.
1. maintenance	1.	1.	
1. evidence		1. 2.	1.

B. READING

Secure your Computer!

Technology has advanced to the point where a large percentage of the population has personal computers. People use these computers in their homes to store personal information, to do on-line banking and bill payment, and to search the Internet. The question arises as to how much security we have when using computers. Are we safe in our own homes when we join a chat room and have interaction with strangers? In a way, aren't we inviting them into our homes and lives? There is increasing evidence that using the Internet opens us up to unwanted attacks. It is, therefore, important to use software that provides security from viruses and alerts us to someone hacking into our personal files. This software must have constant maintenance because new viruses and new ways to break into computers are constantly being found.

C. COMPREHENSION CHECK

Exercise 1

Refer to the previous reading and use the context to guess the meanings of the words below. Then match the words to their definitions. Do NOT use a dictionary.

___ 1. security	A.	words or objects that support the truth; proof
___ 2. technology	B.	communication between people by looks, words, or actions
___ 3. interaction	C.	keeping something in good condition
___ 4. maintenance	D.	protection from danger or loss
___ 5 evidence	E.	science used in practical applications

Exercise 2

Yes or No? Answer the questions with YES or NO.

___ 1. Is <u>security</u> a priority of most governments?

___ 2. Is <u>technology</u> advanced in the United States?

___ 3. Is there <u>interaction</u> between the nations of the world?

___ 4. Is it important to keep up with <u>maintenance</u> on your car?

___ 5. Is there <u>evidence</u> to support the idea that there is life on the moon?

D. WORD STUDY

Exercise 1

Consider the meanings of **secure, security, insecure,** and **insecurity** in a psychological setting.

1.	secure (adj) – sure, confident
2.	security (n) – confidence in one's ability
3.	insecure (adj) – lacking confidence in one's ability
4.	insecurity (n) – a lack of confidence in one's abilities

Write some causes and effects of security and insecurity.

	security	insecurity
causes:		
effects:		

Exercise 2
Choose the correct word form for each blank.

1. Because she grew up in a family that couldn't exhibit love, she has a lot of

   _____.

   a. insecurities   b. secure   c. securely

2. Today's _____ advances make worldwide communication easier.
   a. technology   b. technologically   c. technological

3. The mark of a good language teacher is an _____ classroom.
   a. interactively   b. interacting   c. interactive

4. They had a strong marriage due to the efforts they made to _____ their
   relationship.
   a. maintenance   b. maintain   c. maintaining

5. The confused professor had _____ not prepared for the class.
   a. evidently   b. evidential   c. evident

E. USING WORDS IN COMMUNICATION
Exercise 1 - Lists
1. List three ways technology affects your life.
2. List three examples of evidence used in a court of law.
3. List three things you have to maintain.
4. List three interactions with people you have had recently.
5. List three ways in which you feel secure.

Exercise 2
Working with a partner, give a definition of the underlined word in your own words. Then paraphrase the sentence. (Say the sentence again using your own words.)

1. Campus security efforts have increased following the early morning attacks on
   custodians.

2. Technology can be a blessing or a curse.

3. The substantial evidence against the man led to his conviction.

4. Maintenance of a long-distance relationship requires diligence on both parts.

5. Scientists have observed interaction between animals and deduced that they have the
   ability to communicate.

Lesson 4

A. WORD FAMILIES

Study the five word families below and then fill in the word form chart. The undelined word forms at the top of the list are the most commonly used forms in academic texts.

concept	element	policy	region	significant
/ˈkɑnˌsɛpt/	/ˈɛləmənt/	/ˈpɑləsi/	/ˈridʒən/	/sɪgˈnɪfəkənt/
conception	elemental		regional	significance
conceptual			regionally	signify
conceptualize				significantly
conceptually				insignificant

Exercise - Word Form Chart

NOUN	VERB	ADJECTIVE	ADVERB
1. concept 2.	1.	1.	1.
1. element		1.	
1. policy			
1. region		1.	1.
1.	1.	1. significant 2.	1.

B. READING

Shop 'Til You Drop

In what <u>region</u> of the United States can you find the largest enclosed shopping and entertainment complex? Is it the West Coast? Is it the Southeast? No, they have their own attractions there, but to attract people to the very cold central northern U.S., nothing works better than a mall with a roller coaster, upscale shopping, bargain prices, and wonderful food. The <u>concept</u> is to create an indoor wonderland that brings people from around the world, and they do it at The Mall of America. This mall makes a very <u>significant</u> contribution to Minnesota's state revenues because of the large number of people who visit and spend money there. One <u>element</u> for children is the enormous, blown-up Snoopy, sitting outside of Knott's Camp Snoopy. The mall is open every day, except Thanksgiving or Christmas. The <u>policy</u> is to be closed on those days so that employees can enjoy time with their families.

C. COMPREHENSION CHECK
Exercise 1
Refer to the previous reading and use the context to guess the meanings of the words below. Then match the words to their definitions. Do NOT use a dictionary.

___ 1. concept   A. a part, aspect
___ 2. element   B. a general idea
___ 3. policy   C. a geographical area of a country
___ 4. region   D. important
___ 5. significant   E. a rule or group of rules for doing business

Exercise 2
Choose the word that is different in meaning.

1. concept	idea	belief	difficulty
2. aspect	part	element	whole
3. rule	regulation	desire	policy
4. area	building	location	region
5. essential	important	significant	trivial

D. WORD STUDY
Exercise 1
Many words in word families have a significantly different meaning from the root. Consider these examples.

1. concept (n) - a general idea that usually includes other ideas.
2. conception (n) - the creation of life
3. conception (n) - a beginning

4. element (n) - a part, aspect
5. elemental (adj) - basic, fundamental

Read the following sentences and fill in the blank with the correct word from the words listed above.

1. The most negative _____ of the project is its high cost.
2. Water is an _____ part of our bodies.
3. Since the _____ of this business, he has worked to maintain his integrity.
4. Democracy is a _____ to which many nations subscribe.
5. At _____, the genes come together to make a unique individual.

Exercise 2
Consider this idiomatic usage of the word **element**.

> When the avid skier visited Colorado, she was really <u>in her element</u>.
>
> Having grown up on a farm, the young man felt completely <u>out of his element</u> in Los Angeles.

1. What does it mean to be <u>in one's element</u>?

   _____

2. What does it mean to be <u>out of one's element</u>?

   _____

E. USING WORDS IN COMMUNICATION
Exercise 1

With a partner, discuss the following:

1. What are some <u>policies</u> you would like to change about the high school that you attended? How about the school you are attending now? How can you affect those <u>policies</u>?

2. What are some <u>elemental</u> needs in your life? What <u>elements</u> of your life would you like to change?

3. What are some moral <u>concepts</u> that you really feel strongly about? What are some that you can't agree with?

4. Describe the different <u>regions</u> in your country. What are the <u>regional</u> people, customs, foods, and climates like?

5. Who are the most <u>significant</u> people in your life? What is their <u>significance</u> to you? How have they affected your life <u>significantly</u>?

REVIEW

Find the 20 vocabulary words from this unit in the puzzle below.
Words may be horizontal, vertical, diagonal or backward.

T	E	C	H	N	O	L	O	G	Y	H	T	E	S	A
C	Q	T	O	F	T	T	S	P	N	N	X	V	O	T
P	A	S	V	N	I	P	O	U	A	O	Z	I	N	A
R	O	B	E	D	S	S	E	C	C	A	I	D	O	D
E	Q	L	E	C	I	U	I	C	S	O	F	E	I	K
G	U	R	I	T	N	F	M	E	N	T	F	N	T	R
I	C	E	I	C	I	A	L	E	X	O	W	C	C	T
O	U	V	W	N	Y	E	N	E	R	N	C	E	A	N
N	E	J	G	A	C	H	T	E	C	D	J	R	R	E
W	E	I	A	T	X	D	L	N	T	S	G	V	E	M
P	S	Y	T	I	R	U	C	E	S	N	X	N	T	E
E	T	A	I	R	P	O	R	P	P	A	I	U	N	L
D	E	S	I	G	N	Y	E	V	R	U	S	A	I	E
N	X	L	P	V	D	N	B	H	I	O	P	C	M	Z
R	I	E	J	X	N	W	M	C	M	V	M	S	F	E

appropriate   design   maintenance   select
concept   element   policy   significant
consumer   evidence   positive   survey
credit   focus   region   technology
data   interaction   security   text

Unit 4

Words

administration	distinction	item	remove
authority	economic	legal	research
complex	feature	previous	resource
computer	indicate	principle	specific
consistent	interpretation	reliance	structure

Readings

Who is in the White House?
Beauty at What Cost
People vs. Animals
Greenhouse Effect?

Strategies and Skills

Word Forms
- Word family chart
- Word form selection

Comprehension Check
- Matching definitions
- Understanding and using words in context
- Matching synonyms

Word Expansion
- Collocations
- Multiple meanings
- Prefixes

Interactive Speaking Practice
- Sentence completion
- Listing
- Paraphrasing
- Summarizing

ACADEMIC WORD POWER

LESSON 1

A. WORD FAMILIES

Study the five word families below. Then fill in the word form chart. The underlined word forms at the top of the list are the most commonly used forms in academic texts.

<u>authority</u>	<u>administration</u>	<u>consistent</u>	<u>indicate</u>	<u>previous</u>
/əˈθɔrəti/	/ədˌmɪnəˈstreɪʃən/	/kənˈsɪstənt/	/ˈɪndəˌkeɪt/	/ˈprɪviəs/
authoritative	administrate	consist	indication	previously
	administrative	consistency	indicative	
	administrator	consistently	indicator	
	administratively	inconsistent		

Exercise - Word Form Chart

NOUN	VERB	ADJECTIVE	ADVERB
1. authority		1.	
1. administration 2.	1.	1.	1.
1.	1.	1. consistent 2.	1.
1. 2.	1. indicate	1.	
		1. previous	1.

B. READING

Who is in the White House?

Does the political party of the current president <u>indicate</u> what kind of laws might be passed during the next four years? Some people say yes. They believe that if the <u>previous</u> <u>administration</u> was Democrat, and the current one is Republican, then great changes will occur. Other people believe that the president's office doesn't hold that much <u>authority</u> regarding laws and that the two parties have more or less <u>consistent</u> plans of action. Either way, whatever plan the president has, it can't be put into action without the cooperation of the U.S. Congress.

C. COMPREHENSION CHECK

Exercise 1

Refer to the reading above and use the context to guess the meanings of the words below. Then match the words to their definitions. Do NOT use a dictionary.

    ____ 1. authority   A. one that came before

    ____ 2. administration   B. expertise, power, control

    ____ 3. consistent   C. in accord with, repeated in the same way

    ____ 4. indicate   D. control of business, management

    ____ 5. previous   E. to show, to mean or symbolize

Exercise 2

Complete each sentence with the most suitable word.

previous   administration   authority   indicate   consistently

1. I think that the _____ administration would handle this situation differently from the current one.

2. It's always easier to criticize the people with _____ rather than to propose one's own solution to the problem.

3. His quiet personality doesn't _____ what he is really thinking or feeling.

4. Rules should be applied _____ if they are meant to be taken seriously.

5. The school's _____ is now focusing on ways to retain students.

D. WORD STUDY

Exercise 1

Cross out an item (a word or expression) that DOES NOT go with the underlined word. In each list, one or two items may be crossed out.

1. An <u>administration</u>
   makes rules
   hires employees
   supervises people
   controls business
   strives for failure

2. He has had <u>previous</u>
   experience
   relationships
   nonsense
   failures
   planets

3. The president of a company has the <u>authority</u>
   to give raises
   to declare war
   to evaluate company goals
   to fire employees
   to change company policies

4. These facts <u>indicate</u>
   that he is innocent
   a new dance
   I was correct
   your hometown
   nothing

5. We have <u>consistent</u>
   ideas
   water
   rules
   values
   air

Exercise 2

Fill in the blank in each sentence with the correct word form.

1. If you witness a crime, you should contact the _____.
   a. authorities   b. authoritative   c. authority

2. The company was looking for an _____ assistant.
   a. administrator   b. administrate   c. administrative

3. Rules must be applied _____ for them to be thought of as fair.
   a. consistency   b. consisting   c. consistently

4. Paranoia and extremes of depression and happiness are usually _____ of a mental illness such as Schizophrenia.
   a. indicative   b. indicate   c. indicator

5. Oil prices that had _____ been high fell due to the decrease in demand.
   a. previous   b. previously

E. USING WORDS IN COMMUNICATION
Exercise

Repeat and complete the following sentences.

1. The <u>administration</u> of a democratic country can be described as…

2. A position of <u>authority</u> I would like to hold is…

3. If someone wants to <u>indicate</u> how he/she feels about me, he/she should…

4. My <u>previous</u> educational experiences include…

5. A goal I have <u>consistently</u> strived for is…

LESSON 2

A. WORD FAMILIES
Study the five word families below. Then fill in the word form chart. The underlined word forms at the top of the list are the most commonly used forms in academic texts.

feature (2X)	item	economic	distinction	reliance
/ˈfitʃər/	/ˈaɪtəm/	/ˌɛkəˈnɑmɪk/	/dɪˈstɪŋkʃən/	/rəˈlaɪəns/
featured	itemize	economy	distinct	reliable
	itemized	economical	distinctive	reliability
	itemization	economics	distinctively	reliably
		economist	distinctly	rely
		economically	indistinct	reliant
		uneconomical		unreliable

Exercise - Word Form Chart

NOUN	VERB	ADJECTIVE	ADVERB
1. feature	1.	1.	
1. item 2.	1.	1.	
1. 2. 3.		1. economic 2. 3.	1.
1. distinction		1. 2. 3.	1. 2.
1. reliance 2.	1.	1. 2. 3.	1.

B. READING

Beauty at What Cost?

If you could change a <u>feature</u> of your body, what would it be? Would you change your eyelids, your stomach, or your chin? In the past, cosmetic surgery was only available for people of high <u>economic</u> <u>distinction</u>, especially movie stars. These people could also afford to buy items, like hair extensions, breast or chin implants, and sculptured fingernails. Now the cost of these <u>items</u> and of plastic surgery has come down so much that even people of average means can afford to make changes in their appearances. However, is there another cost? Why is there such a <u>reliance</u> on physical looks for determining self-worth? The cost is for you to decide.

C. COMPREHENSION CHECK
Exercise 1
Refer to the previous reading and use the context to guess the meanings of the words below. Then match the words to their definitions. Do NOT use a dictionary.

___ 1. feature	A. difference
___ 2. items	B. an important part or characteristic
___ 3. economic	C. related to the study of how society uses resources
___ 4. distinction	D. needing someone or something for support or help
___ 5. reliance	E. a general term for things or products

Exercise 2
True or False? Write T or F in the blanks provided.

___ 1. Many newspapers <u>feature</u> the comics on the front page.
___ 2. A mall has few <u>items</u> to buy.
___ 3. The <u>economic</u> situation in Europe is generally stable.
___ 4. There is no <u>distinction</u> between a white lie (a harmless lie) and a malicious lie (a hurtful lie).
___ 5. The current world economy has a heavy <u>reliance</u> on oil.

D. WORD STUDY
Exercise 1
Some words have the same form in noun or verb form. The words also may have many different meanings. Consider the word **feature**.

---

1. feature (n) – an important part or characteristic of a product or service

2. features (n) – the mouth, chin, eyes, nose, etc. of the human face

3. feature (n) – an important article in a newspaper or magazine
      (Note: We can also say feature film or feature-length movie.)

4. feature (v) - to advertise as important, to highlight, to promote

---

Use the above definitions to choose the appropriate meaning and form of the word. Put the number of the definition in the blank provided and write the word in the next blank. Be sure to change verb forms if necessary.

___ 1. Being related, they share many common _____.
___ 2. Each night, restaurants like to _____ some special dishes at special prices.
___ 3. An effective salesman will point out the _____ of whatever product he or she is trying to sell.
___ 4. These days in the movie theater, there might be 10 – 15 minutes of previews before the _____ film begins.
___ 5. The congressman was disturbed to see the _____ about him in the tabloid.

Exercise 2

Prefixes are often used to change the meaning of a word.
Consider the two prefixes used in this unit. Both prefixes mean **not**.

> un-
>
> in-

In your own words, write a definition of the following vocabulary.
Do not use the root word (economical, reliable, distinct) in your definition.

1. uneconomical _____

2. unreliable _____

3. indistinct _____

Now put the words into the correct sentence.

1. It's difficult to meet deadlines on projects when one works with
   _____ coworkers.

2. Living far from work or school is very _____ due to the amount
   of gas necessary and the need for a reliable car.

3. The witness tried to give a detailed description of the man, but the artist's sketch
   turned out to be _____. It looked like any other person.

4. Fancy restaurants are great for special occasions but _____ for
   everyday meals.

E. USING WORDS IN COMMUNICATION
Exercise

With a partner, discuss these questions.

1. What are your best <u>features</u>? What are your worst <u>features</u> in your opinion, and how
   would you change them?
2. What <u>items</u> do you always take when you travel? Why are these <u>items</u> so important
   to you?
3. Discuss some <u>distinctions</u> between you and your best friend's personalities. What are
   the major <u>distinctions</u>? What are some minor ones?
4. Who do you <u>rely</u> on the most in your life? Who <u>relies</u> on you? Do you think you are
   a <u>reliable</u> person? Why or why not?
5. Are you interested in <u>economics</u>? Describe the current <u>economic</u> situation of the
   world. How can the <u>economy</u> be improved in your opinion?

LESSON 3

A. WORD FAMILIES

Study the five word families below. Then fill in the word form chart. The underlined word forms at the top of the list are the most commonly used forms in academic texts.

research(2X)	resource	specific	legal	complex
/ˈriˌsertʃ/	/ˈriˌsɔrs/	/spəˈsɪfɪk/	/ˈligəl/	/kəmˈplɛks/
researcher	resourceful	specification	legally	complexity
		specifically	legality	
		specificity	illegal	
		specifics	illegally	
		specify		

Exercise - Word Form Chart

NOUN	VERB	ADJECTIVE	ADVERB
1. research 2.	1.		
1. resource		1.	
1. 2. 3.	1.	1. specific	1.
1.		1. legal 2.	1. 2.
1.		1. complex	

B. READING

People vs. Animals

When a new drug is developed, how do we know if it's safe? How is it tested? The answer to those questions is <u>research</u>. Numerous studies are done on any drug that will be used by humans before the Food and Drug Administration will approve it. For years, animals have been the main <u>resource</u> in testing these drugs for safety. The researcher must subject animals to a <u>specific</u> amount of the drug for a <u>specific</u> amount of time to see what the results will be. This practice has brought countless benefits to human society. However, organizations, such as People for the Ethical Treatment of Animals, question the validity of this practice. They want to make it illegal to use animals in this way, but currently it is <u>legal</u>. If it becomes illegal, how will drugs be tested? This is a very <u>complex</u> problem that involves the question: Who is more important, animals or people?

C. COMPREHENSION CHECK
Exercise 1
Refer to the previous reading and use the context to guess the meanings of the words below. Then match the words to their definitions. Do NOT use a dictionary.

____ 1. research   A. related to the law
____ 2. resource   B. exact, definite, unique
____ 3. specific   C. complicated
____ 4. legal   D. a study of information, an inquiry
____ 5. complex   E. a useful thing

Exercise 2
Cross out the word that does not belong in each group

1. resources   goods   lack   people
2. exact   specific   unique   usual
3. required   lawful   legal   wished
4. complex   detailed   simple   complicated
5. research   fiction   survey   data

D. WORD STUDY
Exercise 1
Many words in English have multiple meanings.
Consider these meanings of the noun **resource.**

1.   resource – useful things
2.   resources – money, funds
3.   resource – a useful tool in finding something, especially information

Write the number of the correct meaning in the blank before each sentence.

____ 1. Our country is rich in natural <u>resources</u>, such as, oil, gold, and farm land.
____ 2. The college library is an important <u>resource</u> for learning.
____ 3. A thesaurus is a <u>resource</u> that all writers should have.
____ 4. His family has the <u>resources</u> necessary to buy a vacation home.
____ 5. One of our best <u>resources</u> at this firm is the talented people we have working for us.

Exercise 2
Circle the correct choice(s) according to the collocations of the underlined words. For each item, at least one choice is correct, but sometimes two or all choices are correct.

1. His life goal is to _____ <u>research</u>.
   a. make   b. conduct   c. do

2. It is <u>legal</u> _____ a gun in Texas.
   a. to own   b. owning   c. own

3. This tool is <u>specific</u> _____ that kind of work.
   a. to   b. for   c. in

4. It is a <u>complex</u> _____.
   a. cat   b. problem   c. piece of paper   d. situation

5. We don't have the <u>resources</u> _____ anything.
   a. for accomplishment   b. to accomplish   c. accomplishing

E. USING WORDS IN COMMUNICATION
Exercise 1

1. List three <u>resources</u> you can find in the United States.
2. List three activities that are <u>illegal</u> in most countries.
3. List three problems <u>specific</u> to developing countries.
4. List three <u>complex</u> world problems.
5. List three types of <u>research</u>.

Exercise 2
Working with a partner, give a definition of the underlined word in your own words. Then paraphrase the sentence. (Say the sentence again, using your own words.)

1. The results of the <u>research</u> supported the scientist's hypothesis.
2. The diversity of <u>resources</u> in the world is constantly being diminished.
3. Stop speaking in generalities, and give me some <u>specific</u> information on the topic.
4. What society deems as <u>legal</u> has been proven to change.
5. The <u>complexity</u> of the law makes it impossible to interpret without a lawyer.

LESSON 4

A. WORD FAMILIES

Study the five word families below. Then fill in the word form chart. The underlined word forms at the top of the list are the most commonly used forms in academic texts.

computer	structure (2X)	remove	interpretation	principle
/kəmˈpyutər/	/ˈstrʌktʃər/	/rəˈmuv/	/ɪnˌtɜrprəˈteɪʃən/	/ˈprɪnsəpəl/
compute	structured	removal	interpret	principled
computation	structural	removable	interpretive	unprincipled
computerized	structurally			
computable	restructure			
computational	unstructured			

Exercise - Word Form Chart

NOUN	VERB	ADJECTIVE	ADVERB
1. computer 2.	1.	1. 2. 3.	
1. structure	1. 2.	1. 2. 3.	1.
1.	1. remove	1.	
1. interpretation	1.	1.	
1. principle		1. 2.	

B. READING

Greenhouse Effect?

Is the earth getting warmer? According to statistics, it is. The earth's surface temperature has increased by one-half of a degree to one degree Fahrenheit since the late nineteenth century. A comparison of data from the past to data from the present using a <u>computer</u> makes the difference clear. However, scientists don't agree on the <u>interpretation</u> of this data. Some believe it means that global warming is occurring. Others believe it is the natural cycle of warming and cooling that the earth is going through. Other data show that the earth's <u>structure</u> has also changed. Sea level has risen over the past century. Whether global warming is occurring or not, most agree on the <u>principle</u> of the need not to pollute the environment. Since the rising level of carbon dioxide seems to affect this problem directly, activities with CO_2 need to be <u>removed</u> from daily lives as much as possible. It will be a difficult change, but it may be the key to solving the problem.

C. COMPREHENSION CHECK
Exercise 1
Refer to the previous reading and use the context to guess the meanings of the words below. Then match the words to their definitions. Do NOT use a dictionary.

___ 1. computer	A.	taken away, eliminated, dismissed
___ 2. structure	B.	an electronic device that stores and processes information
___ 3. removed	C.	the way parts are organized, a building
___ 4. interpretation	D.	a standard, guide to behavior, rule
___ 5. principle	E.	an explanation, decision about what something means

Exercise 2
True or False? Write T or F in the blanks provided.

____1. Two people can have different <u>interpretations</u>.

____2. <u>Principles</u> can't be taught in school.

____3. A damaged <u>structure</u> needs to be repaired for safety reasons.

____4. Police can <u>remove</u> cars that are parked illegally.

____5. <u>Computers</u> aren't useful for storing information.

D. WORD STUDY
Exercise
Choose the correct word form and write it in the blank of each sentence.

1. After the civil engineer added reinforcements to the bridge, it was
    _____ sound.
    a. structured   b. structurally   c. restructure

2. If you need to use a word processor, you can go to the _____ center
    on campus.
    a. compute   b. computation   c. computing

3. The _____ of asbestos is a complex and dangerous process.
    a. removal   b. removed   c. removable

4. You shouldn't _____ what I say by your cultural standards, or we
    might have a misunderstanding.
    a. interpret   b. interpretive   c. interpretation

5. He was a very _____ young man who relied on what his religion had
    taught him about right and wrong.
    a. principle   b. unprincipled   c. principled

E. USING WORDS IN COMMUNICATION

Exercise 1

Reread the paragraph from this lesson. After two minutes, close your book and summarize the paragraph to your partner. Try to use as many vocabulary words as possible.

Exercise 2

With a partner, discuss the following:

1. Body language has different <u>interpretations</u> from culture to culture. How are crossed arms <u>interpreted</u> by you? Have you ever <u>misinterpreted</u> someone's gestures? Has your body language ever been <u>misinterpreted</u>?

2. How have <u>computers</u> changed our lives? Think of the differences in academic, industrial, and governmental settings.

3. Have you ever had a tooth <u>removed</u>? Who <u>removed</u> it? Why was the <u>removal</u> necessary? How can we keep our teeth from needing to be <u>removed</u>?

4. How did you learn your <u>principles?</u> (from parents, school, religion, friends) Do you consider yourself a <u>principled</u> person? Why are some people <u>unprincipled</u>?

5. Some people like to have a lot of <u>structure</u> in their lives. For example, they like to follow a strict routine instead of being spontaneous. Do you prefer a <u>structured</u> or <u>unstructured</u> life? Why?

REVIEW

Unscramble the sentences and put the words in the correct order to make complete, logical sentences. Write the correct sentences below the scrambled sentence. Underline the vocabulary words from this unit in each sentence.

1. scandals. / The Thomas Jefferson administration / had / many

    _____

2. very / Her / test scores / consistent. / always / are

    _____

3. a siren, / If you / indicates / hear / it / a tornado / that / approaching. / is

    _____

4. found / She / job / her / so / quit. / she / unsatisfying, / previous

    _____

5. earn / In order to / one / do / must / research. / a PHD,

    _____

6. teachers, / hold / Policemen, / parents / and / positions of / all / authority.

    _____

7. has / The USA / on / heavy / oil. / foreign / a reliance

    _____

8. were / great / prosperity / The 90's / a time / of / economic / in the USA.

    _____

9. interpretations / the film / are / of / Our / distinct.

    _____

10. specific / The student / provide more / examples in / her composition. / has to

    _____

UNIT 5

WORDS

analysis	estimate	institute	purchase
aspect	export	legislation	regulation
category	financial	obtain	resident
contract	function	period	strategy
distribution	impact	primary	transfer

READINGS

School Uniforms
Washington D.C.: Old and New
Why the Pain?
From Bean to Chocolate

STRATEGIES AND SKILLS

Word Forms
- Word family chart
- Word form selection

Comprehension Check
- Matching definitions
- Identifying synonyms
- Understanding and using words in context

Word Expansion
- Collocations
- Grammar applications
- Multiple meanings

Interactive Speaking Practice
- Sentence completion
- Role play
- Listing
- Paraphrasing

ACADEMIC WORD POWER

LESSON 1

A. WORD FAMILIES

Study the five word families below. Then fill in the word form chart. The underlined word forms at the top of the list are the most commonly used forms in academic texts.

purchase (2X)	strategy	impact (2X)	financial	estimate (2X)
/'pɜrtʃəs/	/'strædədʒi/	/'ɪmˌpækt/	/fəˈnænʃəl/	/'ɛstəˌmeɪt/
purchaser	strategic		finance	estimated
purchasing	strategically		finances	estimation
	strategist		financially	overestimate
			financier	underestimate

Exercise - Word Form Chart

NOUN	VERB	ADJECTIVE	ADVERB
1. 2.	1. purchase	1.	
1. strategy 2.		1.	1.
1. impact	1.		
1. 2	1.	1. financial	1.
1. 2.	1. estimate 2. 3.	1.	

B. READING

School Uniforms

Some schools have decided to adopt school uniforms. There are both positive and negative reactions to such policies. Parents complain that they must <u>purchase</u> an expensive uniform with all the parts to follow regulations. The truth, however, is that it's still more economical to buy a few uniforms than to buy all the different clothes and shoes that a child going to a school without uniforms needs. School officials say that requiring uniforms is a good <u>strategy</u> to decrease violence and theft while increasing discipline. Not only parents but also students feel the <u>impact</u> of the policy. Some students complain that they want to be able to exhibit their own styles. Others appreciate that a person's <u>financial</u> status or gang affiliation is not apparent when everyone is wearing the same clothes. School officials <u>estimate</u> that it will help students concentrate more on their studies and avoid peer pressure.

C. COMPREHENSION CHECK
Exercise 1
Refer to the reading above and use the context to guess the meanings of the words below. Then match the words to their definitions. Do NOT use a dictionary.

___ 1. purchase	A. related to money
___ 2. strategy	B. to buy
___ 3. impact	C. a plan to achieve some goal
___ 4. financial	D. to make a judgment, calculate
___ 5. estimate	E. effect

Exercise 2
Which word does not belong?

1. buy	acquire	purchase	sell
2. preparation	spontaneity	plan	strategy
3. cause	impact	effect	result
4. financial	money	gift	cash
5. throw	estimate	calculate	guess

D. WORD STUDY
Exercise
These are some common collocations for the words in this unit.

financial institution	strategic oil reserve	fair estimate
purchasing power	direct impact	

Circle the letter of the correct answer for these collocations.
1. An example of a <u>financial institution</u> would be....
   a. a bank
   b. a restaurant
   c. a university

2. Why do we have a <u>strategic oil reserve</u>?
   a. to raise the price of gasoline
   b. to increase manufacturing
   c. to ensure that we will have oil in times of crisis

3. If someone says, "that's a <u>fair estimate</u>," it means...
   a. She totally disagrees with your calculation
   b. She thinks your guess is quite accurate
   c. She wants to make her own estimation

4. Which currency has the most <u>purchasing power</u>?
   a. the Mexican peso
   b. the Russian ruble
   c. the American dollar

5. The construction of a new airport has a <u>direct impact</u> on...
   a. the national economy
   b. a nearby residential area
   c. schools in neighboring states

E. USING WORDS IN COMMUNICATION
Exercise 1
Repeat and complete the following sentences.

1. I enjoy <u>purchasing</u>...
2. Some recent news that has had an <u>impact</u> on me is...
3. My <u>estimation</u> of this city is...
4. In order to be <u>financially</u> healthy, I must...
5. My <u>strategy</u> for learning English in the future is...

Exercise 2
Role Play - You and a business partner are planning to open a clothing store. You need to make decisions about how you will run the business and your strategy for success. Use the words in this unit and create a dialog to present to the class.

purchase   **impact**   **strategy**   **estimate**   **financial**

LESSON 2

A. WORD FAMILIES

Study the five word families below. Then fill in the word form chart. The underlined word forms at the top of the list are the most commonly used forms in academic texts.

regulation	aspect	institute (2X)	resident	legislation
/ˌrɛgyəˈleɪʃən/	/ˈæspɛkt/	/ˈɪnstəˌtut/	/ˈrɛzədənt/	/ˈlɛdʒɪsˌleɪʃən/
regulate		institution	reside	legislate
regulating		institutional	residence	legislative
deregulate		institutionalize	residential	legislator
deregulation		institutionalized		legislature
regulatory		institutionally		

Exercise - Word Form Chart

NOUN	VERB	ADJECTIVE	ADVERB
1. regulation 2.	1. 2.	1. 2.	
1. aspect			
1. 2.	1. institute 2.	1. 2.	1.
1. resident 2.	1.	1.	
1. legislation 2. 3.	1.	1.	

B. READING

Washington DC: Old and New

    Washington, D.C. is the capital of the United States and, therefore, a place of great importance. Tourists flock there to see famous buildings such as, the Washington Monument, the Lincoln Memorial, and the Capitol Building. The Capitol Building is the place where all federal legislation is introduced, revised, and either passed or abandoned. Residents of Washington, D.C. can boast that the President of the United States lives in their neighborhood. It is interesting to note that the White House changes with each new president that lives there. The new first family has the right to institute changes within the house to make the time there more comfortable for them. However, if visitors want to go to the White House, there are many regulations about when, how, long, and where exactly they can go. It only makes sense since this is where the President and his family reside. Most Americans are familiar with these features, but there is another aspect of this interesting city that they may not know. Washington, D.C. has the largest number of ".com" Internet addresses in the U. S.

C. COMPREHENSION CHECK
Exercise 1
Refer to the previous reading and use the context to guess the meanings of the words below. Then match the words to their definitions. Do NOT use a dictionary.

___ 1. regulations   A. a feature, a part of something
___ 2. aspect   B. to begin, to initiate
___ 3. institute   C. rules
___ 4. legislation   D. people who live in an area
___ 5. residents   E. a proposed law or laws, the act of making laws

Exercise 2
Fill in the blank with the correct word from Exercise 1. Change the word form if necessary.

1. Passing _____ for a new trade agreement will take time.

2. What _____ of the advertising campaign still need to be discussed?

3. Since we _____ the new rule, fewer people have been late to work.

4. The State Board of Health makes many_____ about the food, cleanliness, and water in restaurants and food stores.

5. The _____ of the city elected a new mayor.

D. WORD STUDY
Exercise 1
Circle the word(s) that go with the underlined word. One or more possibilities may be correct.

1. Radio and television are regulated _____ the Federal Communication Commission.
   a. by   b. for   c. to

2. I disagree with several aspects _____ the proposal.
   a. of   b. in   c. for

3. He is a resident _____ San Francisco.
   a. to   b. of   c. by

4. That bill is _____ legislation.
   a. new   b. revised   c. handsome

5. We need to institute _____ .
   a. a new ordinance   b. very comprehensive   c. the plan

Exercise 2

Many English words have several meanings. Consider these different meanings of the nouns **institute** and **institution**.

> 1. institute - an organization, especially one for education or research
> 2. institution - an organization that helps people in the area of health, education, or work
> 3. institution - a function in society, i.e. marriage
> 4. institution - something that is a tradition; someone that is a necessary or longtime part of an organization

Chose the meaning of the word which is used in the sentences below and write 1, 2, 3, or 4 in the blank provided.

___ 1. The Massachusetts Institute of Technology is a very prestigious school.

___ 2. His mental disorder forced him to live in a mental institution.

___ 3. The two couples have made an institution of skiing together every winter. They have skied together every January since they were in their twenties.

___ 4. That institution helps people get off welfare and find jobs.

___ 5. Slavery was an institution that was abolished.

E. USING WORDS IN COMMUNICATION

Exercise 1

With a partner, discuss these questions.

1. What aspects of your current school do you enjoy the most? What aspects do you dislike?

2. Are there any new regulations that you think should be instituted at this school.

3. Describe what you know about the legislative process in the United States.

4. Would you like to become a permanent resident of another country? If you live in the United States, in which state would you chose to reside?

5. What kind of regulations did your parents expect you to follow when you were growing up? Which ones did you think were unfair? Which ones were good for you? Why do you think they wanted to regulate your activities?

Exercise 2

You and two partners are on a university housing committee. This committee is revising the regulations for students living in a dormitory. Discuss what you think are the five most important regulations for dormitory residents. For example, no alcohol can be consumed in a dormitory. Discuss also what aspects of the regulations will be the most difficult to institute. Try to use the following vocabulary from this lesson:

regulations	aspects	institute	resident

LESSON 3

A. WORD FAMILIES

Study the five word families below. Then fill in the word form chart. The underlined word forms at the top of the list are the most commonly used forms in academic texts.

obtain	analysis	function (2X)	transfer	distribution
/əb'teɪn/	/ə'næləsɪs/	/'fʌŋkʃən/	/'trænsfər/	/ˌdɪstrɪ'byuʃən/
obtainable	analyze	functional	transfer	distribute
unobtainable	analyst	functionally	transferable	distributional
	analytic	functioning	transference	distributor
	analytical			distributive
	analytically			redistribute
				redistribution

Exercise - Word Form Chart

NOUN	VERB	ADJECTIVE	ADVERB
	1. obtain	1. 2.	
1. analysis 2.	1.	1. 2.	1.
1. function	1.	1. 2.	1.
1. 2.	1. transfer	1.	
1. distribution 2. 3.	1. 2.	1. 2.	

B. READING

Why the Pain?

Pain is the body's way of protecting itself. Can you imagine what would happen if a large rock were crushing your foot, and you didn't know it? You wouldn't move your foot from harm's way. The system in your body responsible for this job is the nervous system. The <u>distribution</u> of nerve cells, called neurons, goes throughout your entire body. The body has 100 billion of these cells. These neurons <u>obtain</u> information from the environment and <u>transfer</u> that data to the central nervous system, which sends it on to the brain. The <u>function</u> of the brain at this point is to do an <u>analysis</u> and decide the appropriate response. For example, the brain might think, "Hey, that rock is going to destroy my toes if I don't pull my foot away!" The brain then sends back a message to the foot that it feels pain, and you jump away to inspect the damage to your foot. Luckily, at this point, the brain releases chemicals called endorphins, which help reduce the pain.

C. COMPREHENSION CHECK
Exercise 1
Refer to the previous reading and use the context to guess the meanings of the words below. Then match the words to their definitions. Do NOT use a dictionary.

___ 1. obtain	A. to move from one place to another
___ 2. analysis	B. to acquire, to get
___ 3. function	C. work done to find facts or solutions, a study
___ 4. transfer	D. a dealing out, supplying, spreading out
___ 5. distribution	E. performance of a task, work

Exercise 2
Yes or No? Answer the questions with YES or NO.

___ 1. Can a visa be <u>obtained</u> at a consulate?
___ 2. Is an <u>analysis</u> a simple explanation?
___ 3. Does your brain <u>function</u> well?
___ 4. Can professors <u>transfer</u> knowledge to students?
___ 5. Does <u>distribution</u> of goods mean keeping them all in one place?

D. WORD STUDY
Exercise
Choose the correct word form for each blank.

1. Scientists believe that one day space travel for common people will be _____.
   a. unobtainable   b. obtain   c. obtainable

2. With an _____ mind, one can become very successful.
   a. analytical   b. analysis   c. analyst

3. This tool is highly _____ in many applications.
   a. function   b. functionally   c. functional

4. As time progresses, it's easy to see a _____ of blame from one party to the next.
   a. transfer (v)   b. transference   c. transferable

5. After doing market research, we can see that it's necessary to _____ our product line quickly to avoid losing sales.
   a. redistribute   b. distributional   c. distributive

E. USING WORDS IN COMMUNICATION
Exercise 1

1. List three methods of <u>distribution</u>.
2. List three ways to <u>transfer</u> money.
3. List three items you have <u>obtained</u> recently.
4. List three machines you have which <u>function</u> well.
5. List three problems in the world which need to be <u>analyzed</u> carefully.

Exercise 2
Work with a partner to read these sentences. Give a definition of the underlined word in your own words. Then paraphrase the sentence. (Say the sentence again, using your own words.)

1. Without a thorough <u>analysis</u> of the situation, it is impossible to make a decision.
2. Although he was born with birth defects, he is highly <u>functional</u>.
3. It is difficult to interrupt the <u>distribution</u> of illegal drugs in the USA.
4. The difficulty of <u>obtaining</u> a working visa depends on the type of work and country of origin.
5. When a country has a military government, the <u>transfer</u> of power is often violent.

LESSON 4

A. WORD FAMILIES
Study the five word families below. Then fill in the word form chart. The underlined word forms at the top of the list are the most commonly used forms in academic texts.

category	contract (2X)	export (2X)	primary	period
/ˈkætəˌgɔriz/	/ˈkɑnˌtrækt/	/ɪkˈspɔrt/	/ˈpraɪˌməri/	/ˈpɪriəd/
categorize	contractor	exporter	primarily	periodic
categorization				periodical
				periodically

Exercise - Word Form Chart

NOUN	VERB	ADJECTIVE	ADVERB
1. category 2.	1.		
1. contract 2.	1.		
1. 2.	1. export		
		1. primary	1.
1. period 2.		1.	1.

B. READING

From Bean to Chocolate

Where did chocolate come from? It certainly didn't start out as a soft, dark piece of candy. It started from a bean. There are two categories of cocoa beans: Criollo and Forastero, but the primary group is the Forastero type. It provides 90 percent of all beans. Cocoa beans are grown in countries that lie close to the equator. For example, Venezuela and Ecuador export cocoa beans. The region of West Africa is another exporter. The beans are harvested during two different periods of the year: in May and in October. Then they are exported to a country that has a contract with the country of origin. For example, Switzerland imports beans from a bean- producing county to make their delicious and famous Swiss chocolate. As a matter of fact, Switzerland also leads the world in chocolate consumption!

71

C. COMPREHENSION CHECK
Exercise 1
Refer to the previous reading and use the context to guess the meanings of the words below. Then match the words to their definitions. Do NOT use a dictionary.

___ 1. categories   A. groups or types of things
___ 2. contract   B. to sell in foreign countries
___ 3. export   C. a written agreement
___ 4. primary   D. segments of time
___ 5. periods   E. main, greatest

Exercise 2
True or False. Write T or F in the blank provided.

___ 1. Meat is one of the <u>categories</u> in the four main food groups.
___ 2. The government sometimes makes a <u>contract</u> with a private company to do work.
___ 3. Most countries of the world choose not to <u>export</u>.
___ 4. The <u>primary</u> reason for attending college is to meet a girlfriend or boyfriend.
___ 5. The Great Depression of the 1930s (when the stock market crashed and many people lost their jobs) was a difficult <u>period</u> in US history.

D. WORD STUDY
Exercise 1
Look at the charts below and try to guess the two additional core meanings of the word **contract** in different contexts.

1.

He <u>contracted</u> malaria abroad. You can <u>contract</u> AIDS through a blood transfusion.

2.

When you bend your arms, your muscles <u>contract</u>. To do a sit-up, you must <u>contract</u> your abdominal muscles

What does <u>contract</u> mean in column 1? In column 2?

Are there any similarities between these 2 meanings?

Exercise 2

Consider the following collocations of the word **primary**.

primary school	primary election	primary care	primary concern

Circle the letter of the correct answer for these collocations.

1. If the girl attends <u>primary school</u>, she attends…
   a. grades 10-12
   b. grades 1-6
   c. college

2. During a <u>primary election</u>…
   a. Democrats compete against other Democrats to run in the general election.
   b. Republicans raise money for Democrats.
   c. Democrats fight with Republicans over non-existent issues.

3. A <u>primary care physician</u> is…
   a. a specialist
   b. the first doctor to see you and make referrals to other doctors
   c. the last doctor to see you and pronounce you dead

4. If your <u>primary concern</u> is money, then you might…
   a. work two jobs and try to save money
   b. go to parties on the weekend and buy your friends drinks
   c. volunteer for a non-profit organization

E. USING WORDS IN COMMUNICATION
Exercise 1

With a partner, discuss the following:

1. Is it okay to break a <u>contract</u>? What can happen if you break one? Have you ever made a <u>contract</u> with anyone?

2. Is it good or bad for the world when countries <u>export</u> their products? How can an <u>export</u>/import imbalance hurt a country financially?

3. What is your <u>primary</u> concern these days? Has it changed from when you were younger? What do you <u>primarily</u> think about when you have free time?

4. Give details about an important <u>period</u> in world history. Try to find similarities and differences with the details of historical <u>periods</u> named by your partner.

REVIEW

Match the sentence halves to make sensible, complete sentences.
Say them aloud to a partner.

____ 1. There are many <u>aspects</u>

____ 2. The <u>analyst</u>

____ 3. That country's <u>strategy</u>

____ 4. The <u>categories</u> we put people into

____ 5. <u>Contracts</u>

____ 6. When Alaska became a state in 1959,

____ 7. Governments in different historical <u>periods</u>

____ 8. Big <u>financial</u> institutions

____ 9. The <u>transfer</u> of that employee

____ 10. If the <u>distribution</u> of these items is timely,

A. <u>function</u> to keep people doing what they say they will do.

B. <u>transfer</u> millions of dollars each day.

C. they can be <u>obtained</u> soon.

D. the <u>residents</u> of that area became US citizens.

E. was <u>instituted</u> by the district manager.

F. can <u>impact</u> the way we perceive them.

G. of this <u>legislation</u> that I disagree with

H. often had different <u>regulations</u> based on the circumstances of that time.

I. is to <u>export</u> to developed countries in exchange for financial aid.

J. <u>estimated</u> that the economy would enter a recession.

UNIT 6

WORDS

assessment	income	negative	role
commission	journal	perceive	relevant
construction	labor	potential	sector
establish	location	range	sought
equation	maximum	reaction	theory

READINGS

Drug Abuse: Problems and Solutions
The Next Armani
Michael Jordan's Steakhouse
Work for the Government

STRATEGIES AND SKILLS

Word Forms
- Word family chart
- Word form selection

Comprehension Check
- Matching definitions
- Understanding and using words in context
- Identifying synonyms
- Pairing sentence halves

Word Expansion
- Multiple meanings
- Grammar applications
- Collocations

Interactive Speaking Practice
- Sentence completion
- Finding cause and effect
- Storytelling
- Role play
- Associations

ACADEMIC WORD POWER

LESSON 1

A. WORD FAMILIES

Study the five word families below. Then fill in the word form chart. The underlined word forms at the top of the list are the most commonly used forms in academic texts.

perceive	commission (2X)	income	potential (2X)	role
/pərˈsiv/	/kəˈmɪʃən/	/ˈɪnˌkʌm/	/pəˈtɛnʃəl/	/roʊl/
perception	commissioner		potentially	

Exercise - Word Form Chart

NOUN	VERB	ADJECTIVE	ADVERB
1.	1. perceive		
1. commission 2.	1.		
1. income			
1.		1. potential	1.
1. role			

B. READING

Drug Abuse: Problems and Solutions

Worldwide, most people <u>perceive</u> drug abuse as a problem. That's why the United Nations developed a <u>commission</u> with the task of analyzing the world drug situation and developing proposals for drug control. One such proposal is reducing the drug supply by helping coca or opium poppy producers find other sources of <u>potential income,</u> such as growing other profitable crops. If the supplier's <u>role</u> can be reduced or removed, fewer drugs will be available on the market. The commission hopes that this will be one step in the process of fighting drug abuse.

C. COMPREHENSION CHECK
Exercise 1
Refer to the previous reading and use the context to guess the meanings of the words below. Then match the words to their definitions. Do NOT use a dictionary.

___ 1. perceive		A.	money earned from work or investments
___ 2. commission		B.	a part or job someone (or something) has in a particular situation
___ 3. income		C.	to think of as, to understand, to feel
___ 4. potential		D.	a group of people authorized to do something
___ 5 role		E.	possible

Exercise 2
Complete each sentence with the most suitable word.

perceive   **commission**   **income**   **potential**   **role**

1. A doctor earns a high _____.

2. Her _____ in the play was small but important.

3. A _____ was set up to look at the city's water problems.

4. Across cultures, different people _____ gestures differently.

5. Because of the warnings about the ice storm, there is a _____ interruption in classes.

D. WORD STUDY
Exercise 1
Many English words have several meanings. Consider the following meanings of the word **commission**.

---

1. commission (n) – an amount of money paid, often to a sales representative, for selling a product or service

2. commission (n) – a group of people authorized to do a task

3. commission (n) – a formal document of acceptance as an officer into the military

4. commission (v) - to set up a group of people as a commission

5. commission (v) – to accept a person as an officer into the military

6. commission (v) – to ask someone to create a piece of art or music

---

Write the number of the correct meaning on the line next to each sentence.

___ 1. The town council created a <u>commission</u> to protect its historical landmarks.

___ 2. Michelangelo was <u>commissioned</u> to paint the Sistine Chapel.

___ 3. Our salespeople work on <u>commission</u> only.

___ 4. The new admiral will be <u>commissioned</u> in a ceremony today.

___ 5. They <u>commissioned</u> a group of scientists to study cloning.

___ 6. The young marine remembered fondly the day she received her <u>commission</u>.

E. USING WORDS IN COMMUNICATION
Exercise 1
Repeat and complete the following sentences.

1. If I have money in the future, I will <u>commission</u> someone to build me...
2. A <u>potential</u> spouse has these characteristics...
3. I want to be <u>perceived</u> as...
4. My <u>role</u> in my family is...
5. In the future, I expect my <u>income</u> will be...

Exercise 2
The phrases listed below contain vocabulary words from the lesson. List possible causes and effects related to these phrases. An example has been done for you.

	Phrase	Causes	Effects
Example:	Potential problem	lack of money	can't pay bills

1. low income

2. traditional female role

3. transportation safety commission

LESSON 2

A. WORD FAMILIES

Study the five word families below. Then fill in the word form chart. The underlined word forms at the top of the list are the most commonly used forms in academic texts.

establish	journal	negative (2X)	range (2X)	theory
/ɪˈstæblɪʃt/	/ˈdʒɜrnl/	/ˈnɛgətɪv/	/reɪndʒ/	/ˈθɪəri/
establishment		negate		theoretical
disestablish		negated		theoretically
disestablishment		negatively		theorize

Exercise - Word Form Chart

NOUN	VERB	ADJECTIVE	ADVERB
1. 2.	1. establish 2.		
1. journal			
1.	1.	1. negative 2.	1.
1. range	1.		
1. theory	1.	1.	1.

B. READING

The Next Armani

What does it take to <u>establish</u> a career in fashion? Would you like to see your clothing designs worn by models posing in famous <u>journals</u> like *Vogue* or walking down a Paris runway? Most employers are looking for designers who have degrees and who know about textiles, fabric, and fashion trends. They desire candidates to have an eye for a wide <u>range</u> of colors and proportions. Designers should also understand the <u>theory</u> of balance and have an appreciation of beauty. Not having at least some of these requirements and skills can have a <u>negative</u> impact on your ability to get started in the fashion industry. However, if you have these skills and natural talents, you could become the next Armani!

C. COMPREHENSION CHECK
Exercise 1
Refer to the reading at the beginning of the unit and use the context to guess the meanings of the words below. Then match the words to their definitions. Do NOT use a dictionary.

_____ 1. range   A. magazines, newspapers, or written record
_____ 2. theory   B. critical, doubtful, against something
_____ 3. establish   C. to prove, find, create
_____ 4. journals   D. an idea, speculation that something is true
_____ 5. negative   E. a variety of ideas, things or products

Exercise 2
True or False? Write T or F in the blanks provided.

_____ 1. In the USA, people have a wide range of political opinions.
_____ 2. Einstein's Theory of Relativity is generally accepted.
_____ 3. A police detective tries to establish the facts in a criminal case.
_____ 4. A dictionary is considered a journal.
_____ 5. A negative person won't have many friends.

D. WORD STUDY
Exercise 1
Cross out one item that does not go with the underlined word.

1. It ranges
   from 64-100 percent
   from hot to cold
   in size
   sharply
   in the bedroom

2. One can debate the Theory of
   The Big Bang
   Evolution
   facts
   Relativity

3. It was established
   in 1954
   by the state of California
   under the house
   to be true
   to be a fact

4. This is a journal of
   medicine
   water
   popular science
   business reports
   law

5. He has a negative
   perception
   opinion
   golf club
   attitude

Exercise 2
Look at the chart below and try to guess the two additional core meanings of the word range in different contexts.

1.

> The test average was 77 percent, but the range was from 50 - 100 percent.
>
> The piano is an instrument with a great range of notes.

2.

> The Rockies are a mountain range in the western U.S.A.
>
> The Alps are a range in Europe

What does range mean in column 1? in column 2?

Are there similarities between these 2 meanings?

E. USING WORDS IN COMMUNICATION
Exercise
Group Activity: Read through the following five words and make sure that everyone understands their meanings. Then make up a story that uses all the words. You can use any word form of the specific word. The story can be about anything. Be creative. Each student in the group must contribute! Talk about the story, and then write it down. Decide who will read it to the class.

establish   range   journal   theory   negative

LESSON 3

A. WORD FAMILIES

Study the five word families below. Then fill in the word form chart. The underlined word forms at the top of the list are the most commonly used forms in academic texts.

location	sought *	relevant	maximum (2X)	equation
/louˈkeɪʃən/	/sɔt/	ˈrɛləvənt/	/ˈmæksəməm/	/ɪˈkweɪʒən/
locate	seek	relevance	maximize	equate
relocate		irrelevant	maximization	
relocation		irrelevance		

* **sought** is the irregular past tense verb form of the base verb **seek**

Exercise - Word Form Chart

NOUN	VERB	ADJECTIVE	ADVERB
1. location 2.	1. 2.		
	1. sought 2.		
1. 2.		1. relevant 2.	
1. 2.	1.	1. maximum	
1. equation	1.		

B. READING

Michael Jordan's Steakhouse

We all know what a phenomenal basketball player Michael Jordan is, but he has added a new career to his resume. He is now the owner of a restaurant. The <u>location</u> of his restaurant is the Grand Central Terminal in New York City. How does an athlete know the most <u>relevant</u> factors in the <u>equation</u> for a successful restaurant? First of all, Jordan <u>sought</u> a great chef. After finding the chef, he bought excellent food and wine. When you put these things together, you get a wonderful meal that can be expensive or reasonable. The <u>maximum</u> cost of a bottle of wine at the steakhouse is 1,400 dollars, but another bottle goes for 30 dollars. Because of good business practices, Michael Jordan's Steakhouse was nominated for best steak in New York in 2000. That's another slam dunk!

C. COMPREHENSION CHECK
Exercise 1
Refer to the previous reading and use the context to guess the meanings of the words below. Then match the words to their definitions. Do NOT use a dictionary.

___ 1. location		A. the place where something is
___ 2. sought		B. a mathematical statement that two amounts are equal
___ 3. relevant		C. the ultimate, most of something
___ 4. maximum		D. looked for
___ 5. equation		E. closely connected, appropriate

Exercise 2
Cross out the word that doesn't belong in each group.

1.	site	place	location	air
2.	sought	looked for	searched	lost
3.	important	relevant	connected	unnecessary
4.	least	most	maximum	largest
5.	formula	comparison	television	equation

D. WORD STUDY
Exercise
Find errors in the following sentences and correct them.

1. The facts presented must are <u>relevant</u> to your argument.　　(1 mistake)

2. To <u>maximum</u> efficiency from a car, it's important to keep the tire pressure at the specified amount.　　(1 mistake)

3. The Galapagos Islands were a great <u>locate</u> for Darwin to study the evolution at different species.　　(2 mistakes)

4. The scientist <u>seeked</u> a solution for the problem.　　(1 mistake)

5. The <u>equation</u> for happiness is combining a success career and a fulfilling personal live.　　(2 mistatkes)

E. USING WORDS IN COMMUNICATION

Exercise 1

You and a partner will be roommates starting next month. You must find a place to live. Create a dialog to share with the class using the words from this unit.

location	seek	maximum	relevant

Consider these questions:

> How will you <u>seek</u> out the place?
> (newspaper, campus organization, recommendation from a friend)
>
> What kind of <u>location</u> do you want?
>
> What is the <u>maximum</u> rent you are willing to pay?
>
> What issues are <u>relevant</u> to your choice?

Exercise 2 - Word Associations

In the chart below, write one word you associate with each of the words from the lesson. Then go around the classroom and find other students with the same associations. Try to find as many different people as possible with the same associations.

seek	
equation	
maximum	
relevant	
location	

LESSON 4

A. WORD STUDY

Study the five word families below. Then fill in the word form chart. The underlined word forms at the top of the list are the most commonly used forms in academic texts.

assessment	sector	reaction	labor (2X)	construction
/əˈsɛsmənt/	/ˈsɛktər/	/riˈækʃən/	/ˈleɪbər/	/kənˈstrʌkʃən/
assess		react	laborious	construct
assessable		reactionary		constructive
reassess		reactive		reconstruct
reassessment		reactor		

Exercise – Word Form Chart

NOUN	VERB	ADJECTIVE	ADVERB
1. assessment 2.	1. 2.	1.	
1. sector			
1. reaction 2.	1.	1. 2.	
1. labor	1.	1.	
1. construction	1. 2.	1.	

B. READING

Work for the Government

People often consider getting a job with the U.S. government, especially in times when unemployment is high. Jobs within the public <u>sector</u> can have many advantages. Usually, the benefits provided by the government are very good. For example, health insurance and dental plans are better than ones that small private companies can offer. The <u>labor</u> force in the public sector is also guaranteed a certain number of holidays and shorter working hours than the private sector. Public sector jobs include both outdoor jobs, like <u>construction</u> of highways and taking care of national parks, and indoor jobs, like teaching at public schools or being an agent in one of the many government offices. The pay may not be high, but after an <u>assessment</u> of the other advantages, a common <u>reaction</u> of people in a tight job market is to apply for a job with the government.

C. COMPREHENSION CHECK

Exercise 1

Refer to the previous reading and use the context to guess the meanings of the words below. Then match the words to their definitions. Do NOT use a dictionary.

___ 1. assessment   A. work, workforce
___ 2. sector   B. an evaluation, analysis
___ 3. reaction   C. a division of society or business
___ 4. labor   D. a response, an answer
___ 5. construction   E. the act of building

Exercise 2

Match the clauses on the left with those that complete them on the right.

___ 1. If you are giving an <u>assessment</u>,   a. anger.
___ 2. The private and business <u>sectors</u>   b. you should be objective.
___ 3. A typical <u>reaction</u> to pain is   c. you can't enter.
___ 4. <u>Labor</u> is expensive in   d. usually pay better than government agencies.
___ 5. If the building is under <u>construction</u>, e. industrialized countries.

D. WORD STUDY

Exercise

These are some common collocations for the words in this unit.

private/public sector	overreaction	labor union
under construction	property assessment	

Circle the letter of the correct answers for these collocations.

1. The <u>private sector</u> is made up of...
   a. for profit organizations
   b. government agencies
   c. transportation services

2. A facility of the <u>public sector</u> is...
   a. a church
   b. the courthouse
   c. a movie theater

3. If a sign reads <u>under construction</u>, it means...
   a. they are constructing a basement
   b. they are building or repairing something inside the area
   c. you can't take pictures of it

4. An <u>overreaction</u> to spilled milk would be…
   a. cleaning it up
   b. leaving it for the cat to drink
   c. crying

5. If my <u>property assessment</u> is low, I will probably…
   a. earn less money off the sale of my home
   b. earn a lot of money off the sale of my home
   c. expect the bank to repossess my home and sell it for me

6. We can expect a <u>labor union</u> to…
   a. stay at home and watch TV
   b. fight for fair wages and safe working conditions
   c. agree with everything that management wants to do

E. USING WORDS IN COMMUNICATION
Exercise 1
With a partner, discuss the following:

1. Would you rather work in the public or private <u>sector</u>? Why?

2. Are <u>labor</u> unions powerful? How do they help <u>laborers</u>?

3. What is a serious problem you've had in your life? How did you <u>react</u> to this problem? In general, are your <u>reactions</u> to problems calm and logical or emotional?

4. Often when major highways and roads are <u>under construction</u> in cities, it causes traffic jams. However, it is necessary to improve the roads. What is the best way <u>to construct</u> new roads and repair old ones? Try to find a solution to this problem.

5. How do teachers <u>assess</u> progress in English classes (multiple choice tests, presentations, essays, etc.)? What method of <u>assessment</u> do you prefer?

REVIEW

Circle words and draw lines between words that you associate with each other. There is not one correct word association, and you may have more than one association with certain words and no associations at all with other words. Think about why you make these associations, and be able to explain them to a partner.

assessment   equation

                        location

potential   relevant

                        commission

income   maximum

                        range

sector   construction

                        journal

negative   reaction

                        seek

established   labor

                        role

perceived   theory

UNIT 7

WORDS

acquisition	document	investment	register
comment	exclude	issue	restrict
consequence	formula	layer	sequence
conduct	fund	link	site
core	initial	philosophy	technique

READINGS

Taking a Deep Breath
Play Fair with Stocks
Burning Fat with Aerobics
Find it on *Ebay*

STRATEGIES AND SKILLS

Word Forms
- □ Word family chart
- □ Word form selection

Comprehension Check
- □ Matching definitions
- □ Understanding and using words in context
- □ Pairing sentence halves
- □ Identifying synonyms

Word Expansion
- □ Multiple meanings
- □ Pronunciation tips
- □ Collocations

Interactive Speaking Practice
- □ Associations
- □ Listing
- □ Sentence completion

ACADEMIC WORD POWER

LESSON 1

A. WORD FAMILIES
Study the five word families below. Then fill in the word form chart. The underlined word forms at the top of the list are the most commonly used forms in academic texts.

exclude	conduct (2X)	technique	initial	site
/ɛkˈskludə/	/kənˈdʌkt/	/tɛkˈnik/	/ɪˈnɪʃəl/	/saɪt/
exclusion			initially	
exclusionary				
exclusionist				
exclusive				
exclusively				
excluded				

Exercise - Word Form Chart

NOUN	VERB	ADJECTIVE	ADVERB
1. 2.	1. exclude	1. 2. 3.	1.
1.	1. conduct		
1. technique			
		1. initial	1.
1. site			

B. READING

Taking a Deep Breath

Psychosomatic illnesses are common in today's society. *Psycho* means "of the mind" and *soma* means "of the body." A psychosomatic illness occurs when the mind creates physical symptoms or makes them worse. One such illness that affects 15 million adults in the U.S. is asthma. The <u>initial</u> cause of an asthma attack may be the sound of a cat meowing (real or not). That sound causes a psychological response. The asthmatic knows that he or she usually has an asthma attack when he or she is near a cat, so the mind begins to alert the body. The next reaction is a tightening in the chest and constricting of the air passageways in the lungs. Now the asthmatic person is having difficulty breathing. Even though the mind creates the problem, the <u>site</u> where the reaction occurs is the lungs. The good news is that asthmatics can learn to <u>conduct</u> themselves in a way that reduces problems. Stress seems to be the biggest factor in causing psychosomatic reactions, so stress must be <u>excluded</u> from their lives as much as possible. One <u>technique</u> for doing this is biofeedback. Biofeedback teaches a person to relax and slow the heart rate and breathing. With this method, people can reduce the emotional causes of psychosomatic illness.

90

C. COMPREHENSION CHECK
Exercise 1
Refer to the previous reading and use the context to guess the meanings of the words below. Then match the words to their definitions. Do NOT use a dictionary.

___ 1. excluded   A. to behave

___ 2. conduct   B. a location, area

___ 3. technique   C. beginning, first

___ 4. initial   D. method, procedure

___ 5. site   E. left out, not included

Exercise 2
Complete each sentence with the most suitable word.

   site   initial   techniques   excluded   conduct

1. When entering a construction _____, it's necessary to wear a hard hat.

2. When in Rome, _____ yourself as the Romans do.

3. Many forms of art require _____ that seem to be inherent rather than learned.

4. The young woman's _____ diagnosis turned out to be completely wrong, which led to ineffective drugs being prescribed.

5. In the USA, we have laws which say that people can't be _____ based on race, religion, disability, sex, or age.

D. WORD STUDY
Exercise
Some words have the same form in noun or verb form. The spelling is the same, but the meaning and pronunciation can be different. Study the meanings of the noun and verb forms of **conduct** below.

---

conduct (n)   /ˈkɑn₁dʌkt/
1. conduct (n) – behavior, comportment
2. conduct (n) – the process of doing something

conduct (v)   /kənˈdʌkt/
3. conduct (v) – to behave
4. conduct (v) – to do something
5. conduct (v) – to direct an orchestra or band

Use the previous definitions of conduct to choose the appropriate meaning and form of the word. Put the number in the first blank. Write the word in the blank in the sentence. Be sure to change verbforms if necessary.

___ 1. He has _____ The London Philharmonic Orchestra for ten years.

___ 2. Good _____ is expected of students in school.

___ 3. The _____ of diplomacy takes a lot of experience to master.

___ 4. She _____ herself in a professional manner during the interview.

___ 5. This store has _____ business in the Boston area for over 50 years.

E. USING WORDS IN COMMUNICATION

Exercise 1

In the chart below, write one word you associate with each of the words from this lesson. Then go around the room and see if anyone has one or more of the same words associated with the vocabulary words. If you find someone who does, sit with that classmate and discuss your associations. If you do not find a student with any of the same associations, choose a partner with whom to discuss your associations.

initial	
site	
technique	
exclude	
conduct	

Exercise 2

Discuss these questions with a partner.

1. What was your underline{initial} feeling about this school?

2. What underline{sites} in the world do you want to see?

3. What underline{techniques} can you teach your partner?

4. Have you ever been underline{excluded} from something? Tell about it.

5. What kind of underline{conduct} is expected from children by parents?

LESSON 2

A. WORD FAMILIES

Study the five word families below. Then fill in the word form chart. The underlined word forms at the top of the list are the most commonly used forms in academic texts.

<u>investment</u>	<u>fund</u> (2X)	<u>document</u> (2X)	<u>consequence</u>	<u>restrict</u>
/ɪn'vɛstmənt/	/fʌnd/	/'dɑkyəmənt/	/'kɑnsə‚kwɛns/	/rə'strɪkt/
invest	funder	documentation	consequent	restricted
investor		documented	consequently	restriction
reinvest				restrictive
reinvestment				restrictively
				unrestricted

Exercise - Word Form Chart

NOUN	VERB	ADJECTIVE	ADVERB
1. investment 2. 3.	1. 2.		
1. fund 2.	1.		
1. document 2.	1.	1.	
1. consequence		1.	1.
1.	1. restrict	1. 2. 3.	1.

B. READING

Play Fair with Stocks

Buying and selling stock can be a quick and easy way to make money. Many people set aside <u>funds</u> for <u>investment</u> in the stock market. However, the federal government <u>restricts</u> the trading of stocks in several ways. One restriction is what is called insider trading. A person is not allowed to trade stocks based on information that was obtained secretly or that was not available to the general public. The <u>consequences</u> for doing this can be devastating. If there is a <u>document</u> or other evidence linking that person to insider trading or securities fraud, going to jail is a real possibility.

C. COMPREHENSION CHECK
Exercise 1

Refer to the previous reading and use the context to guess the meanings of the words below. Then match the words to their definitions. Do NOT use a dictionary.

___ 1. investment A. a sum of money for a specific purpose

___ 2. funds B. money, time, or energy spent in order to gain something

___ 3. document C. the results of doing something

___ 4. consequences D. to limit

___ 5. restrict E. a paper, such as a letter, contract, or record

Exercise 2

Match the clauses on the left with those that complete them on the right.

___ 1. If you make an <u>investment</u>, A. getting a costly ticket.

___ 2. If you destroy a <u>document</u>, B. it sends money to another place.

___ 3. If your parents restrict you C. you don't have as much freedom.

___ 4. One <u>consequence</u> of speeding is D. you hope to gain something.

___ 5. If the bank transfers <u>funds</u>, E. you tear it up.

D. WORD STUDY
Exercise 1

Circle the correct word form for each sentence.

1. Due to his disease, he has a very _____ diet.
   a. unrestricted   b. restriction   c. restricted

2. Consumer confidence dropped this quarter. _____, consumers aren't spending as much money, which negatively affects the economy.
   a. consequent   b. consequently   c. consequence

3. The manager plans to remove his money from high-tech stocks and _____ it in government bonds.
   a. reinvestment   b. investor   c. reinvest

4. You may not enter a foreign country without the proper _____.
   a. documentation   b. documented

5. The university plans to _____ the new project.
   a. funds   b. fund   c. funder

Exercise 2

Consider the following collocations of the words **invest** and **investment**.

invest time	invest money	invest energy
good investment	bad investment	

Yes or No – Read the following sentences and decide if the collocation is used correctly. Write YES or NO in the blank provided.

_____ 1. After retirement, many senior citizens like to <u>invest time</u> in volunteer work.

_____ 2. It doesn't require any funds to <u>invest money</u> in a business venture.

_____ 3. Learning a second language requires you to <u>invest energy</u> in the process.

_____ 4. Most people avoid putting money into a <u>good investment</u>.

_____ 5. When you get twice the money you invested in return, we consider this a <u>bad investment</u>.

E. USING WORDS IN COMMUNICATION
Exercise

Working with a partner, discuss investments. First, make a list of things you both consider to be good investments and things you consider to be bad investments. Then discuss the characteristics of each. What do the items on each list have in common?

<u>good investments</u>   **<u>bad investments</u>**

LESSON 3

A. WORD FAMILIES

Study the five word families below. Then fill in the word form chart. The underlined word forms at the top of the list are the most commonly used forms in academic texts.

layer (2X)	link (2X)	philosophy	register (2X)	comment (2X)
/ˈleɪər/	/lɪŋk/	/fəˈlɑsəfi/	/ˈrɛdʒɪstər/	/ˈkɑˌmɛnt/
layered	linkage	philosopher	registered	commentary
		philosophical	registration	commentator
		philosophically	deregister	
		philosophize		

Exercise - Word Form Chart

NOUN	VERB	ADJECTIVE	ADVERB
1. layer	1.	1.	
1. 2.	1. link		
1. philosophy 2.	1.	1.	1.
1. 2.	1. register 2.	1.	
1. 2. 3.	1. comment		

B. READING

Burning Fat with Aerobics

Everyone wants to be healthy and attractive. One way to do that is through aerobic exercise. Experts link aerobic exercise to stronger cardiovascular systems, which help people do more work for a longer duration and recover more quickly from activity. Aerobic instructors share the philosophy that there is no better workout than aerobics, and that it should be done three to five times a week for maximum results. This can help burn layers of fat off the body, which will definitely register on the scales. Some instructors comment, however, that a person cannot choose where the fat will come off. While a person exercises, the blood carries fat to be used as energy, and it generally comes off in the reverse order that it was put on.

C. COMPREHENSION CHECK
Exercise 1
Refer to the previous reading and use the context to guess the meanings of the words below. Then match the words to their definitions. Do NOT use a dictionary.

___ 1. layer   A. something that is placed on or between other things
___ 2. link   B. general truth or belief
___ 3. philosophy   C. to remark, to give opinion
___ 4. register   D. to connect
___ 5. comment   E. to show or indicate

Exercise 2
Cross out the word that doesn't belong in each group

1.	layer	part	section	total
2.	connect	break	attach	link
3.	beliefs	ideas	philosophy	lie
4.	list	register	unknown	record
5.	say	remark	comment	silence

D. WORD STUDY
Exercise
Study the multiple meanings and uses of the vocabulary words, and then do the exercise that follows.

---

1. register (v) - to write one's name on an official list, such as a voter list or school's student list
2. register (v) - to include, indicate one's ideas or opinion
3. register (v) - to show or indicate (on instruments or faces)
4. register (n) - a range of sound made by a voice or instrument

---

5. link (n) - one connection in a series, such as a ring in a chain.
6. link (n) - part of a communication or transport system
7. link (n) - relationship
8. link (v) - to connect
9. link (n) - "weak link" : a connection likely to break

---

10. layer (n) - a coating, covering
11. layer (n) - a thickness, usually one of several
12. layer (v) - to arrange in layers

Write YES if the underlined word is used correctly or NO if it is used incorrectly.

_____ 1. The pastry chef created a 5 <u>layer</u> cake for the wedding.

_____ 2. If you're hungry, you can find some leftover dinner in the <u>register</u>.

_____ 3. The reporter was <u>linked</u> to the main TV station via satellite phone.

_____ 4. In the 1980s it was the fashion to <u>layer</u> many different shirts, such as turtle necks, polo shirts, and oxfords.

_____ 5. A <u>weak link</u> is essential to a growing business.

_____ 6. The doctor became concerned when the scale <u>registered</u> only 110 pounds for the fully grown man.

E. USING WORDS IN COMMUNICATION

Exercise 1

On a sheet of paper, write down several words that you associate with each of these five keywords. When you finish, cut up the lists and give them to your partner. She/He will give you hers/his. Try to place the associated words under the correct keywords. Compare and discuss.

register   link   layer   philosophy   comments

Exercise 2

Repeat and complete the following sentences.

1. I am a <u>registered</u> voter in…

2. My <u>philosophy</u> in life is…

3. When someone <u>comments</u> negatively on my work, I feel…

4. I see a <u>link</u> between happiness and…

5. A <u>layer</u> of dust on someone's furniture tells me…

LESSON 4

A. WORD FAMILIES

Study the five word families below. Then fill in the word form chart. The underlined word forms at the top of the list are the most commonly used forms in academic texts.

acquisition	core (2X)	sequence (2X)	formula	issue (2X)
/ˌækwəˈzɪʃən/	/kɔr/	/ˈsikwəns/	/ˈfɔrə/	/ˈɪʃu/
acquire		sequential	formulate	
		sequentially	formulation	
			reformulate	
			reformulation	

Exercise - Word Form Chart

NOUN	VERB	ADJECTIVE	ADVERB
1. acquisition	1.		
1. core	1.		
1. sequence	1.	1.	1.
1. formula 2. 3.	1. 2.		
1. issue	1.		

B. READING

Find it on *Ebay*

Where can you buy that hard-to-find object you've been looking for? The <u>acquisition</u> of anything you can imagine, except humans and body parts, takes place on a daily basis on the Internet. You can buy everything from baby <u>formula</u> to cars on *ebay*. *Ebay* is an Internet site for buying and selling by everyday common people. Every transaction follows a certain <u>sequence</u>. If you are selling, you put your product on *ebay*'s site for a specific period of time. People make bids of certain dollar amounts on the product. When the auction is finished, which usually takes one to two days, the product is sold to the highest bidder. Then it's the winner's responsibility to contact the seller and send payment. Next, the seller must send the item to the winner. If a person doesn't act in a fair manner, and you have <u>issues</u> with the way the person acted, you can register a complaint that is attached to that person's selling name for everyone to see. Millions of people around the world use *ebay* occasionally, but there is also a <u>core</u> group of *ebay* professionals. Those people actually use *ebay* as a source of income by selling products from their homes for companies.

C. COMPREHENSION CHECK
Exercise 1
Refer to the previous reading and use the context to guess the meanings of the words below. Then match the words to their definitions. Do NOT use a dictionary.

___ 1. acquisition   A. a fixed combination of ingredients
___ 2. core   B. topics or matters of concern
___ 3. sequence   C. the center of anything
___ 4. formula   D. a purchase, process of obtaining something
___ 5. issues   E. a connected series of acts

Exercise 2
True or False? Write T or F in the blanks provided.

___ 1. The earth's <u>core</u> is molten rock.
___ 2. Only Einstein can understand mathematical <u>formulas</u>.
___ 3. The decision making process is a step-by-step <u>sequence</u>.
___ 4. The <u>acquisition</u> of an island is a common occurrence.
___ 5. There are many serious <u>issues</u> facing the world today.

D. WORD STUDY
Exercise 1
These are some common collocations for the words in this unit.

business acquisition	pressing issue	sequential order
rotten to the core (idiomatic)	formula for success (idiomatic)	

Circle the letter of the correct answers for these collocations.

1. Bill Gates' <u>formula for success</u> might be...
   a. staying up late at night to create new programs
   b. using his good luck charms
   c. hard work, creative employees, and stopping the competition

2. If we say a person is <u>rotten to the core</u>, it means...
   a. he/she always helps his/her friends
   b. he/she is totally corrupt or bad
   c. he/she likes to eat apples so much that he/she eats the rotten core.

3. An example of a <u>business acquisition</u> would be...
   a. IBM selling a part of its business to an international company
   b. two giant companies merging to form a new company
   c. AT&T buying excite.com at a good price

4. If there is a <u>pressing issue</u>...
   a. it must be discussed as soon as possible
   b. it isn't anything important
   c. it is a matter that can be postponed until much later

5. If something must be done in <u>sequential order</u>, it means...
   a. any order is fine
   b. the steps must be followed in a particular order
   c. the order will be decided by whoever is doing the task

Exercise 2

Many English words have several meanings. Consider these 5 meanings of the word **issue**.

> 1. issue (v) - to give or send out, distribute
> 2. issue (v) - to give or provide in a formal or official way
> 3. issue (n) - a topic or matter of concern
> 4. issue (n) - a dated copy of a magazine or newspaper
> 5. issue (n) - a special supply of something made available at a certain time

Put the correct number of the meaning in each sentence in the blank provided.

___ 1. We don't have plans to discuss that <u>issue</u> during today's meeting.
___ 2. The Division of Motor Vehicles <u>issues</u> driver's licenses.
___ 3. Between 1941 and 1945, the White House <u>issued</u> news about the war on almost a daily basis.
___ 4. You can find old <u>issues</u> of that journal in the archives at the university library.
___ 5. An <u>issue</u> of Thanksgiving stamps will be available at the post office this month.

D. USING WORDS IN COMMUNICATION
Exercise 1

With a partner, discuss the following:

1. Should students be required to memorize mathematical and scientific <u>formulas</u> in school? How can these <u>formulas</u> help them in life?

2. What are the most pressing <u>issues</u> internationally today? How can these <u>issues</u> be resolved?

3. If you have a lot of money in the future, what will you <u>acquire</u>? Would you like to <u>acquire</u> art, property, or expensive cars? Tell your partner about your dream <u>acquisitions</u>.

4. Name some people in history that were <u>rotten to the core</u>. Describe what they did that made them seem so rotten. Are there any current leaders in the world that are <u>rotten to the core</u>? Why do you consider them that way?

5. Put your daily activities into <u>sequential order</u>, and then describe them to your partner.

REVIEW

Match the definition on the right with the appropriate key word on the left.
Write the letter in the blank provided.

___ 1.   acquisition   a. money

___ 2.   core   b. coating

___ 3.   fund   c. opinions

___ 4.   comments   d. center

___ 5.   documents   e. method

___ 6.   initial   f. purchase

___ 7.   layer   g. outcome

___ 8.   link   h. combination

___ 9.   consequences   i. concerns

___ 10. excluded   j. beliefs

___ 11. investment   k. behavior

___ 12. philosophy   l. beginning

___ 13. conduct   m. left out

___ 14. formula   n. area

___ 15. issue   o. steps

___ 16. register   p. time, money, or energy spent

___ 17. restricted   q. indicate, show

___ 18. sequence   r. papers

___ 19. site   s. limited

APPENDICES

A. ACADEMIC WORD LIST INDEX
B. ROOTS, PREFIXES, SUFFIXES

APPENDIX A
WORD LIST INDEX

Academic Word List Index

The 140 target words studied in this book come from the Academic Word List (see Introduction, page ix for a description of the AWL). The four volumes of Academic Word Power cover 560 of the 570 words on the AWL. Below is a complete, alphabetical list of the AWL. The numbers indicate the volume, unit and page number where the word is introduced.

Word	v.u.pg	Word	v.u.pg	Word	v.u.pg
abandon	3.7.90	aspect	1.5.65	coincide	4.4.51
abstract	3.3.40	assemble	4.2.18	collapse	4.6.78
academy	2.2.18	assess	1.6.85	colleague	4.1.2
access	2.7.92	assign	3.7.101	commence	4.5.64
accommodate	4.5.70	assist	1.1.8	comment	3.7.96
accompany	3.7.101	assume	3.1.5	commission	1.6.76
accumulate	4.1.8	assure	4.6.78	commitment	2.5.75
accurate	2.7.94	attach	2.6.89	commodity	4.6.81
achieve	1.2.18	attain	4.2.24	communicate	
acknowledge	3.4.46	attitude	2.2.21	community	1.1.2
acquire	1.7.100	attribute	3.1.5	compatible	4.5.60
adapt	3.6.84	author	2.5.75	compensate	2.2.24
adequate	2.6.89	authority	1.4.46	compile	4.5.64
adjacent	4.4.46	automate	3.3.32	complement	4.7.96
adjust	2.5.66	available	1.1.8	complex	1.4.53
administrate	1.4.46	aware	2.4.56	component	4.1.11
adult	3.2.24	behalf	4.5.70	compound	4.3.35
advocate	3.4.46	benefit	1.1.8	comprehensive	3.4.49
affect	1.2.18	bias	3.3.34	comprise	3.5.66
aggregate	3.5.60	bond	4.1.2	compute	1.4.56
aid	3.2.24	brief	2.5.69	conceive	4.7.90
albeit	4.7.99	bulk	4.3.32	concentrate	2.7.94
allocate	3.6.81	capable	3.2.18	concept	1.3.41
alter	2.1.8	capacity	2.6.86	conclude	1.1.11
alternative	2.3.37	category	1.5.71	concurrent	4.7.90
ambiguous	3.4.52	cease	4.4.46	conduct	1.7.90
amend	3.1.8	challenge	2.1.5	confer	4.1.11
analogy	4.4.48	channel	4.1.8	confine	4.6.76
analyze	1.5.68	chapter	1.2.18	confirm	3.3.32
annual	2.1.11	chart	4.3.40	conflict	3.1.2
anticipate	4.1.11	chemical	4.2.18	conform	3.4.52
apparent	2.4.60	circumstance	2.2.21	consent	2.7.100
append	4.3.32	cite	3.4.46	consequent	1.7.93
appreciate	3.2.24	civil	2.5.69	considerable	2.4.50
approach	1.2.18	clarify	3.6.81	consist	1.4.46
appropriate	1.3.32	classic	4.3.32	constitute	
approximate	2.2.28	clause	2.4.60	constant	2.3.43
arbitrary	4.3.38	code	4.2.21	contract	1.5.71
area	1.1.11	coherent	4.6.76	constrain	3.1.8

Word	v.u.pg	Word	v.u.pg	Word	v.u.pg
constrain	1.6	differentiate	3.6.74	evaluate	1.2.21
consult	2.6.86	dimension	2.6.86	eventual	3.4.52
consume	1.3.32	diminish	4.3.35	evident	1.3.38
contact	4.3.32	discrete	2.7.100	evolve	2.4.57
contemporary	3.3.34	discriminate	3.4.52	exceed	3.3.32
context	1.218	displace	4.5.70	exclude	1.7.90
contradict	3.5.66	display	2.5.75	exhibit	3.7.97
contrary	4.2.21	dispose	3.6.77	expand	4.3.40
contrast	2.2.24	distinct	1.4.50	expert	2.6.83
contribute	2.3.40	distort	4.7.93	explicit	3.5.63
controversy	4.7.93	distribute	1.5.68	exploit	4.6.76
convene	2.5.75	diverse	3.3.34	export	1.5.71
converse	4.1.2	document	1.7.93	external	2.3.46
convert	3.6.84	domain	3.5.60	extract	3.6.77
convince	4.4.46	domestic	2.4.53	facilitate	4.3.32
cooperate	3.2.27	dominate	2.3.37	factor	1.1.2
coordinate	2.2.94	draft	2.6.86	feature	1.4.50
core	1.7.100	drama	3.7.90	federal	4.2.27
corporate	4.2.24	duration	4.2.27	fee	2.5.66
correspond	2.3.43	dynamic	3.4.55	file	4.1.5
couple		economy	1.4.50	final	1.1.14
create	1.2.21	edit	3.5.69	finance	1.5.62
credit	1.3.32	element	1.3.41	finite	3.6.77
criteria	2.7.104	eliminate	3.2.21	flexible	2.5.75
crucial	3.4.49	emerge	2.3.34	fluctuate	3.7.97
culture	1.1.2	emphasis	1.2.21	focus	1.3.32
currency	4.4.54	empirical	3.6.74	format	4.4.51
cycle	2.2.21	enable	4.1.5	formula	1.7.100
data	1.3.35	encounter	4.3.40	forthcoming	4.5.84
debate	2.2.18	energy	2.1.2	foundation	3.3.37
decade	3.2.21	enforce	3.1.2	found	4.3.40
decline	2.4.50	enhance	3.3.34	framework	2.2.28
deduce	2.2.28	enormous	4.4.54	function	1.5.68
define	1.1.11	ensure	2.1.5	fund	1.7.93
definite	3.6.77	entity	4.2.18	fundamental	2.3.37
demonstrate	2.1.5	environment	1.1.5	furthermore	2.6.89
denote	4.2.27	equate	1.6.82	gender	3.2.18
deny	3.2.18	equip	3.2.21	generate	3.1.11
depress	4.6.76	equivalent	2.5.72	generation	2.2.28
derived	3.1.5	erode	4.4.46	globe	3.3.34
design	1.3.35	error	2.2.24	goal	2.1.8
despite	2.1.8	establish	1.6.79	grade	4.2.21
detect	3.7.94	estate		grant	2.4.57
deviate	4.4.51	estimate	1.5.62	guarantee	3.2.18
device	4.5.64	ethic	4.3.40	guideline	3.3.32
devoted	4.6.78	ethnic	2.4.53	hence	4.1.8

Word	v.u.pg	Word	v.u.pg	Word	v.u.pg
hierarchy	3.6.74	internal	2.2.24	minimum	2.5.69
highlight	3.2.27	interpret	1.4.56	ministry	4.1.2
hypothesis	2.5.72	interval	3.5.66	minor	1.1.5
identical	3.2.24	intervene	3.4.46	mode	3.4.55
ideology	3.7.90	intrinsic	4.6.81	modify	2.3.43
ignorance	2.6.83	invest	1.7.93	monitor	2.6.80
illustrate	2.1.11	investigate	2.3.43	motive	3.1.2
image	2.3.37	invoke	4.6.81	mutual	4.7.90
immigrate	2.2.21	involve	1.2.24	negate	1.6.79
impact	1.5.62	isolate	3.1.8	network	2.4.53
implement	2.7.97	issue	1.7.100	neutral	3.3.40
implicate	4.2.27	item	1.4.50	nevertheless	3.1.5
implicit	4.7.90	job	2.1.8	nonetheless	4.4.54
imply	2.1.11	journal	1.6.79	norm	4.4.51
impose	2.7.104	justify	2.6.83	normal	1.1.5
incentives	3.5.60	label	2.1.2	notion	2.5.72
incidence	3.6.74	labor	1.6.85	notwithstanding	4.7.90
incline	4.7.99	layer	1.7.96	nuclear	4.6.78
income	1.6.76	lecture	2.5.72	objective	2.4.60
incorporate	3.6.74	legal	1.453	obtain	1.5.68
index	4.1.5	legislate	1.5.65	obvious	2.2.24
indicate	1.4.46	levy	4.5.64	occupy	2.2.18
individual	1.2.21	liberal	2.5.66	occur	1.1.5
induce	4.5.60	license	2.3.40	odd	4.5.60
inevitable	4.5.70	likewise	4.2.18	offset	4.7.96
infer	3.2.24	link	1.7.96	ongoing	4.3.38
infrastructure	4.6.78	locate	1.6.82	option	2.3.46
inherent	4.4.48	logic	2.4.57	orient	2.5.66
inhibit	3.6.84	maintain	1.3.38	outcome	2.1.5
initial	1.7.90	major	1.2.24	output	
initiate	3.5.69	manipulate	3.7.94	overall	2.4.57
innovate	3.3.37	manual	4.4.46	overlap	4.4.54
input		margin	2.7.104	overseas	4.1.2
insert	3.7.101	mature	4.3.35	panel	4.2.21
insight	4.3.38	maximize	1.6.82	paradigm	4.1.11
inspect	3.3.32	mechanism	4.2.18	paragraph	
instance	2.4.60	media	3.2.21	parallel	2.7.104
institute	1.5.65	mediate	4.7.93	parameter	3.1.8
instruct	2.6.86	medical	2.3.34	participate	1.1.2
integral	4.7.96	medium	4.3.35	partner	1.2.24
integrate	2.4.50	mental	2.1.11	passive	4.5.70
integrity	4.2.21	method	1.1.8	perceive	1.6.76
intelligence	2.5.69	migrate	3.1.11	percent	1.2.24
intense	3.7.97	military	4.5.60	period	1.5.71
interact	1.3.38	minimal	4.6.81	persist	4.6.76
intermediate		minimize	3.2.21	perspective	2.6.86

Word	v.u.pg	Word	v.u.pg	Word	v.u.pg
phase	2.2.28	recover	3.1.10	simulate	3.4.55
phenomenon	3.4.55	refine	4.5.67	site	1.7.90
philosophy	1.7.96	regime	4.2.27	so-called	4.5.67
physical	1.1.5	region	1.3.41	sole	3.2.18
plus	4.2.24	register	1.7.96	somewhat	3.4.52
policy	1.3.41	regulate	1.5.65	source	2.1.2
portion	4.3.35	reinforce	3.7.101	specific	1.4.53
pose	4.5.67	reject	2.3.34	specify	4.6.84
positive	1.3.32	relax	4.1.5	sphere	4.2.24
potential	1.6.76	release	3.5.60	stable	2.5.66
practitioner	4.7.99	relevant	1.6.82	statistic	2.5.72
precede	3.3.40	reluctance	4.3.38	status	2.6.80
precise	2.6.80	rely	1.4.50	straightforward	4.6.84
predict	2.1.5	remove	1.4.56	strategy	1.5.62
predominant	3.7.90	require	1.2.27	stress	2.1.2
preliminary	4.4.51	research	1.4.53	structure	1.4.56
presume	3.4.49	reside	1.5.65	style	2.3.37
previous	1.4.46	resolve	2.4.50	submit	3.6.81
primary	1.5.71	resource	1.4.53	subordinate	4.5.60
prime	2.6.80	restrain	4.6.84	subsequent	2.7.100
principal	2.7.94	restrict	1.7.93	subsidy	3.5.66
principle	1.4.56	retain	2.7.97	substitute	2.6.89
prior	3.3.37	reveal	3.1.5	successor	3.3.40
proceed	4.6.84	revenue	2.6.89	sufficient	2.4.57
process	1.2.24	reverse	3.5.63	sum	2.3.40
professional	2.1.2	revise	3.6.81	summary	2.7.104
prohibit	3.5.63	revolution	4.4.48	supplement	4.4.54
project	2.3.34	revise	3.6.81	survey	1.3.35
promote	2.7.97	role	1.6.76	survive	3.5.69
proportion	2.4.53	route	4.7.99	suspend	4.7.93
prospect	3.6.84	scenario	4.7.96	sustain	2.3.34
protocol	4.7.99	schedule	3.2.27	symbol	2.4.60
psychology		scheme	2.7.100	tape	4.1.5
publication	3.5.66	scope	3.6.81	target	2.1.11
publish	2.2.18	section	1.2.27	task	1.2.27
purchase	1.5.62	sector	1.6.85	team	4.2.24
pursue	2.5.69	secure	1.3.38	technical	4.1.8
qualitative	4.6.81	seek	1.6.82	technique	1.7.90
quote	3.3.37	select	1.3.35	technology	1.3.38
radical	3.7.90	sequence	1.7.100	temporary	4.3.38
random	3.2.27	sex		tense	3.4.46
range	1.6.79	series	2.1.8	terminate	3.6.84
ratio	3.1.8	shift	2.7.100	text	1.3.35
rational	3.4.49	significance	1.3.41	theme	3.7.94
react	1.6.85	similar	1.1.11	theory	1.6.79

Word	v.u.pg
thereby	3.7.101
thesis	3.2.27
topic	3.5.69
trace	3.6.77
tradition	1.2.27
transfer	1.5.68
transform	3.4.55
transit	2.3.43
transmit	3.5.63
transport	3.1.11
trend	2.6.83
trigger	4.7.93
ultimate	3.5.63
undergo	4.4.48
underlie	3.1.2
undertake	2.7.94
uniform	3.7.97
unify	4.5.67
unique	3.3.40
utilize	3.1.11
valid	2.2.18
vary	1.2.27
vehicle	3.7.94
version	2.4.53
via	3.7.94
violate	4.6.84
virtual	3.7.97
visible	3.5.80
vision	4.5.67
visual	4.1.8
volume	2.7.97
voluntary	3.5.69
welfare	2.6.83
whereas	4.1.11
whereby	4.7.96
widespread	3.4.49

APPENDIX B
Roots, Prefixes, Suffixes

COMMON ROOTS, PREFIXES AND SUFFIXES IN ACADEMIC VOCABULARY

Academic vocabulary is mainly of Latin or Greek origin, so knowing common Greek and Latin roots, prefixes, and suffixes can be very helpful in learning and remembering academic vocabulary. The following tables list some common roots and affixes along with their meanings and examples. The examples in bold are words from the Academic Word List.

LATIN ROOTS

Roots	Meaning	Examples
act	to do, drive	**interact, compact, extract**
ann, enn	year	**annual,** bicentennial
aqu	water	aquarium, aqueduct
aud	to hear	auditorium, auditor
bell	war	belligerent, bellicose
cede	to go, to yield	**precede,** concede
cent	one hundred	**percent,** centennial
cept, capt, cip, cap, ceive, ceipt	to take hold, grasp	**conceive,** receive, capture
cert	to be sure, to trust	certain, certify
cess, ced	to go, to yield	**process,** successor, cessation
cid, cis	to cut off, be brief, to kill	concise, homicide
circ, circum	around	**circumstance,** circumference
clin	to lean, lie, bend	**decline, incline**
cog	to think, consider	recognize, cognitive
cor, cord, card	heart	coronary, cardiology
corp	body	**corporate,** corpse
cred	to believe, to trust	**credit,** credible
crit, cris	to separate, judge	**criteria,** criticism
culp	fault, blame	culprit, culpable
dic, dict	to say, to speak, to assert	**contradict, predict**
duct, duc	to lead, to draw	**conduct, deduce**
dur	hard, lasting	**duration,** durable
ego	I	egotistical, egocentric
equ	equal, fair	**equation,** equator
fac, fic, fect, fact	to make, do	**facilitate, affect**
fer	to carry, bear, bring	**transfer, infer, confer**
fin	end, limit	**definite, finite, confine**
flu	to flow	**fluctuations,** fluid
form	shape	**uniform , formula, transform**
fort	strong	fortify, fortress
fum	smoke, scent	perfume, fumigate
gen	race, family, kind	**generation, gender**
grad, gress	step, degree, rank	**grade,** gradual
grat	pleasing, thankful	grateful, congratulate
grav, griev	heavy	gravity, grieve, grave
hab	to have, hold, to dwell	habitat, habit
hom	man, human	homicide, homage
init	to begin, enter upon	**initial, initiate**
jur, jus, judic	law, right, judgment	**justify, adjust,** judicial
juven	young	juvenile, rejuvenate
laud	praise	laud, laudable
leg	law	**legal, legislate**
liber	free	**liberal, liberate**

Roots	Meaning	Examples
loc	place	**location, allocate,** local
manu	hand	**manual,** manuscript
med, medi	middle	**medium, mediate,** mediocre
medic	physician, to heal	**medical,** medicine
memor	mindful	memorial, memorable
mon	to remind, advise, warn	**monitor, demonstrate**
ment	mind	**mental,** mentality
migr	to move, travel	**immigration, migration**
mit, mis	to send	**transmit,** submit
mort	death	mortal, mortality
mov, mob, mot	to move	**remove,** mobile, motion
mut	change, exchange	mutate, mutant
nomen, nomin	name, meaning	nominate, synonym
null, nihil, nil	nothing, void	nihilism, nullify
ped	foot	pedestrian, pedestal
pend, pond, pens	to weigh, pay, to consider	**compensate,** pension, pensive
plur, plus	more	**plus,** surplus
port	to carry	**export, transport**
pos	to place, put	**dispose, impose, expose**
pot	powerful	**potential,** potent
prim, prin	first	**primary, prime**
reg, rig, rect	to rule, right, straight	**regulation,** rigid
rupt	to break, burst	disrupt, interrupt, rupture
sacr, secr, sanct	sacred	sacrifice, sanctify
sat, satis	enough	satisfy, satiate
scrib, script	to write	inscribe, subscription
sed, sid, sess	to sit, to settle	sedate, sediment, subside
sent, sens	to feel	sentimental, sense
sequ, secut	to follow, sequence	**consequence, sequence, subsequent**
sumil, simul, sembl	like,	**similar, simulation**
sol, soli	alone, lonely	**solely, isolate**
spec, spect, spic	to see, look at, behold	**perspective, inspect**
spond, spons	to pledge, promise	**respond, correspond**
tac, tic	silent	tacit, taciturn
ten, tain, tent	to hold	**obtain, retain, attain**
tend, tens	to stretch, strive	**tension,** tendon
termin	boundary, limit	**terminate, terminal**
test	to witness, affirm	attest, testify
tract	to pull, draw	**contract, extract**
trib	to allot, give	**distribute, contribute**
vac	empty	evacuate, vacuous
ven, vent	to come	**convention, intervene**
ver	truth	verify, veracity
vers, vert	to turn	**convert, reverse, controversy**
via	way, road	**via,** viaduct
vir	manliness, worth	virile, virtue
vis, vid	to see, look	**visible, revision, visual**
viv, vit	life	vital, vivacious
voc, vok	voice, call	**invoke, vocal, revoke**

Roots	Meaning	Examples
GREEK ROOTS		
anthropo	human being	anthropology, philanthropic
aster, astro	star	asteroid, astronomy
bio	life	biography, biology
chrom	color	chromatic, chromosome
chrono	time	chronology, chronometer
cosmo	world, order, universe	cosmos, cosmopolitan
crac, crat	rule, govern	aristocrat, democracy
dem	people	**demonstrate,** epidemic
derm	skin	dermatology, hypodermic
ethno	nation	ethnic, ethnocentric
eu	good, well	euphoric, euphemism
gam	marriage	monogamy, polygamy
geo	earth	geology, geodynamics
gno, kno	to know	knowledge, diagnostic
graph gram	to write, draw, record	telegraph, telegram
gymno, gymn	athletic	gymnasium, gymnastics
hydro	water	hydrogen, hydroplane
hypno	sleep	hypnosis, hypnotize
hypo	under, below	**hypothesis,** hypodermic
logue, logo	idea, word, speech, reason	**logic, ideological**
meter, metr	measure	**parameters,** metric
micro	small	microscope, microorganism
mim	copy	mimic, mime
mono	one	monogram, monogamy
mor	fool	moron, moronic
morph	form, structure, shape	morphology, metamorphosis
neur, nero	nerve	neural, neurotic
opt	eye	optic, optician
ortho	straight	orthodontist, orthopedics
pan	all	**expansion,** pantheism
path	feeling, disease	sympathy, pathologist
phe	speak, spoken about	prophet, euphemistic
phil, philo	love	**philosophy,** philanthropist
phob	fear	phobia, claustrophobia
phon	sound, voice	telephone, phonograph
photo	light	photosynthesis, photography
pneu	breath	pneumonia, pneumatic
polis, polit	citizen, city, state	political, metropolitan
poly	many	polygamy, polytechnic
pseudo	false	pseudo, pseudonym
psych	mind, soul, spirit	psychic, psychology
pyr	fire	pyromania, pyrotechnic
scope	to see	**scope,** telescope
soph	wise	**philosophy,** sophisticated
sym, syn	together	**symbolic,** synthesize
techn	art, skill	**technical, technology**
tele	at a distance	telescope, telephone
the, them, thet	to place, put	**hypothesis,** epithet
thea, theatr	to see, view	theatre, theatrical
theo	God	**theory,** theology
therm	heat	thermometer, thermal

PREFIXES

Prefix	Meaning	Examples
ab-	from, away from	absent, **abnormal**
ad-	to, motion toward, addition to	**advocate, administrate, adapt**
aero-	air	aerobic, aerospace
a-, an-	without	atonal, anarchy
ante-	before	antecedent, anteroom
anti-	against, opposite, reverse	anti-aircraft, antibiotics
ap-	to, nearness to	**approximate**, appoint
auto-	self	**automatic**, autograph
bene-	good	**benefit**, benefactor
bi-	two	**biannual**, bifocal
co-, con-	together	**community, cooperative, coordination , context**
contra-	against	**contrast, controversy, contradiction**
de-	opposite of, away from, undo	**deduction, decline**
dis-	opposite	**displace, disproportion**
ex-	out, beyond, away from, former	**exclude, export, external**
extra-	outside, beyond, besides	extraordinary, extracurricular
fore-	before	foreword, forecast
hyper-	more than normal, too much	hyperactive, hypersensitive
il-	not	**illegal, illogical**
im-	into	**impact, imply, immigrate**
im-	not	**immature**, imbalance
in-	not	**incapable, indiscreet, inaccurate**
inter-	among, between	**interaction, intervention, interval**
intra-	within	intramural, intrastate
ir-	not	**irrelevant, irrational**
mal-	wrong, bad	malfunction, malpractice
mis-	wrong, bad, no, not	misinterpret, misbehave
non-	not, opposite of	nontraditional, nonconformist
per-	through	**perceive, perspective**
post-	after	postgraduate, postglacial
pre-	before	**precede, previous, preliminary**
pro-	before, for, in support of	**promote**, prologue
pro-	forward	**project, proceed**
re-	back, again	**reassess, recreate, redefine**
retro-	backward	retroactive, retrospect
self-	of the self	self-respect, self-taught
semi-	half, partly	semiformal, semi-circle
sub-	under, beneath	**subordinate**, submarine
sur-	over, above	surcharge, surpass, **survey**
trans-	across, over	**transition, transport**
ultra-	extremely	ultramodern, ultrasonic
un-	not, lack of, opposite	**uninvolved, unreliable, unaware**

SUFFIXES

Suffix	Meaning	Examples
-able, -ible	can, able to	detectable, accessible, flexible
-age	action or process	percentage, linkage, voyage
-al, -ial	of, like, relating to, suitable for	cultural, traditional, potential
-ance	act, process, quality, state of being	maintenance, reliance, assurance
-ant	one who	assistant, participant
-ary	of, like, relating to	temporary, primary, voluntary
-ate	characteristic of, to become	alternate, demonstrate, eliminate
-cle, -icle	small	particle, cubicle
-cy	fact, or state of being	policy, residency
-dom	state or quality of	random, boredom
-ence	act or state of being	evidence, sequence, intelligence
-ent	doing, having, showing	consistent, sufficient, inherent
-er	one who, that which	consumer, achiever
-ery	place for, act, practice of	recovery, robbery
-ess	female	princess, goddess
-ful	full of	stressful, insightful
-ic	relating to, characteristic of	economic, specific, academic
-ify	to make, to cause to be	identify, unify
-ion	act, condition, result of,	conclusion, evaluation
-ish	of or belonging to, characterized by	stylish, selfish
-ism	act, practice, or result of, example	individualism, professionalism
-ity	condition, state of being	security, maturity, stability
-ive	of, relating to, belonging to	negative, alternative, legislative
-ize	make, cause to be, subject to	civilize, energize, finalize
-less	without	ceaseless, jobless
-logue	speech	dialogue, monologue
-logy	study or theory of	psychology, ideology
-ly	every	annually, daily
-ly	in (a specified manner, to a specified extent)	normally, automatically
-ment	action or process	commitment, assessment, adjustment
-ment	state or quality of	refinement, amusement
-ment	product or thing	environment, document
-ness	state or quality of being	awareness, uniqueness, intenseness
-or	one who	minor, actor
-ous	having, full of, characterized by	ambiguous, enormous, erroneous
-ship	state or quality of being	partnership, authorship
-some	like, tending to be	bothersome, noisome
-tude	state of quality of being	attitude, solitude
-y	characterized by	contemporary, voluntary, contrary

Reference:
Elliot, Norbert. Vocabulary Workshop. Austin, Texas: Holt, Rinehart and Winston, 2001.